BOUND

The First Array

BOUND, Volume 1
© 2015 the authors
18 17 16 15   1 2 3 4

BOUND and the Bloof Books Chapbook Series is edited by Shanna Compton
Design & composition: Shanna Compton, shannacompton.com
Cover photograph: Six Cubes, Mohawk Eco Cream i-Tone with glue, Shanna Compton

Published by Bloof Books
www.bloofbooks.com
New Jersey

Bloof Books are printed in the USA by BookMobile. Booksellers, libraries, and other institutions may order direct from us by contacting sales@bloofbooks.com. POD copies are distributed via Ingram, Baker & Taylor, and other wholesalers. Individuals may purchase our books direct from our website, from online retailers such as Amazon.com, or request them from their favorite bookstores.

Please support your local independent bookseller whenever possible.

ISBN-13: 978-0-9826587-8-9
ISBN-10: 0-9826587-8-8
1. American poetry—21st century.   2. Poets, American—21st century.
I. Compton, Shanna   II. Series
∞ This paper meets the requirements of ANSI/NISO Z39.48-1992 (Permanence of Paper).

Contents

13   Jennifer Tamayo: *Poems Are the Only Real Bodies*

41   Pattie McCarthy: *scenes from the lives of my parents*

66   Kirsten Kaschock: *Windowboxing*

105   Hailey Higdon: *Packing*

125   Jared White: *This Is What It Is Like to Be Loved by Me*

151   Becca Klaver: *Nonstop Pop*

187   Notes & Acknowledgments
189   About the Authors
190   Index of Authors, Titles & First Lines
195   Publisher Catalog & Chronology

List of Illustrations

13   Cover: *Poems Are the Only Real Bodies*
21   Photograph: The Sentence
30   Photograph: I Got Emotional
41   Cover: *scenes from the lives of my parents*
66   Photograph: *Windowboxing*
67   Facsimile: Title Page for *Windowboxing*
74   Drawing: Untitled
83   Drawing: Untitled
88   Drawing: Untitled
92   Drawing: Untitled
97   Drawing: Untitled
103   Drawing: Untitled
105   Cover: *Packing*
125   Cover: *This Is What It Is Like to Be Loved by Me*
151   Cover: *Nonstop Pop*

187   Credits included with Notes & Acknowledgments

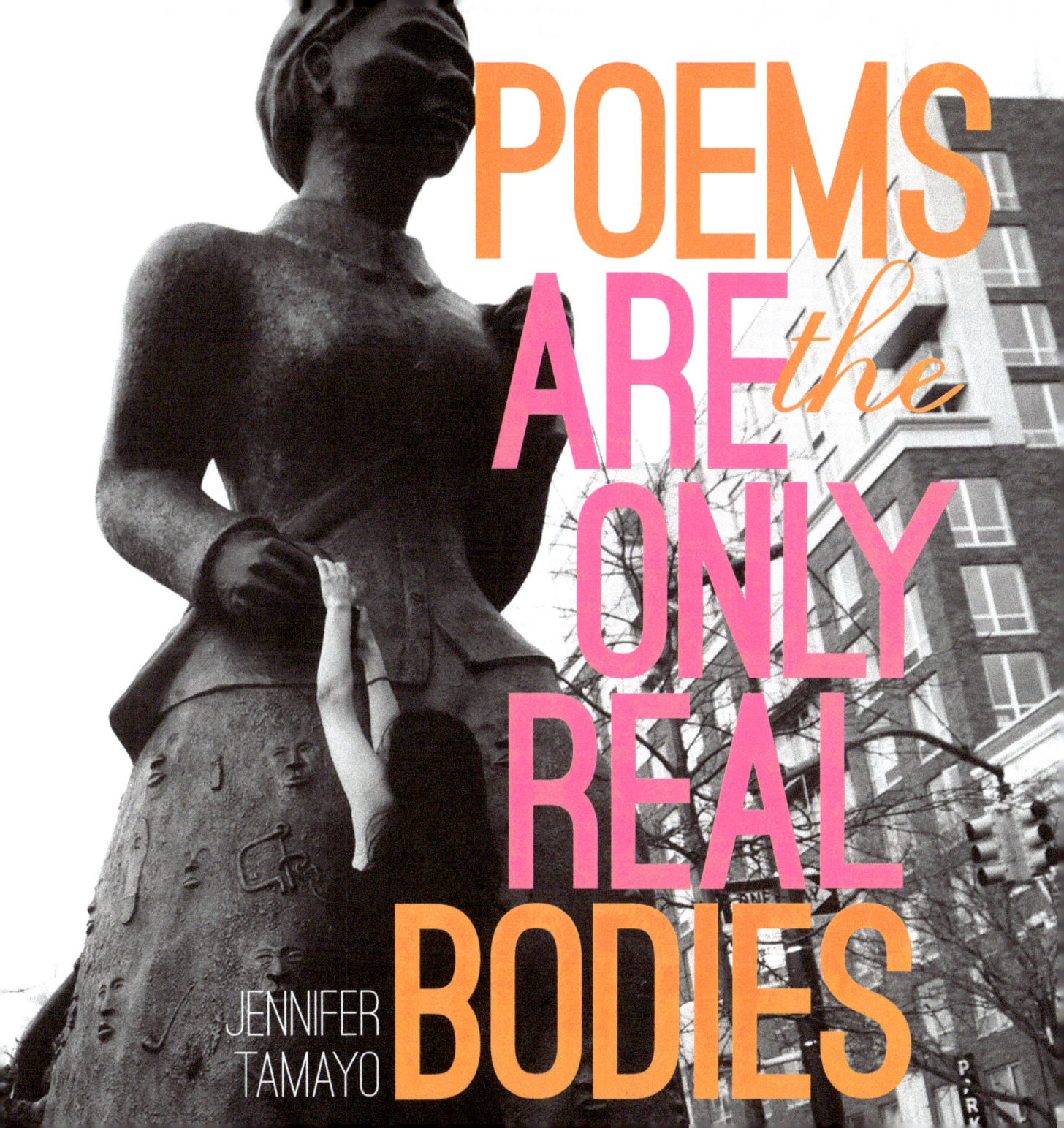

Poems Are the Only Real Bodies
Jennifer Tamayo

7 x 7 inches | 28 pages

80# cream cover | natural white interior
machine zigzag stitch in pink & orange thread

Approximate scale here: 90%

What is happening here is a positioning:

the crack body of history in the membrane of my current happenstance. Here I am! a terror!st. Please know that when I place these arms on you, dear reader, we both corrupt with pleasure. The guttural guh guh guh guh! of

what it means to experience the letter

Dear Harriet Tubman,

How is it to be buried under the singular displeasure of the sentence?

Your life story is depicted in a series of silhouette panels; i.e. the sentence like a sentence. In one, an infant's body. In another, trees surround the figure of the woman shape. Then the marriage. Then the journey. Then the house. Then the deathbed. Then the letters. Harriet, I eat the pink stained tyranny of a sentence for you—get a little bit emo. I get emo near the garbage by the placard. I get emo next the Lay's Potato Chips bag. I get emo-tional around the empty Heineken bottles likes doves in the bushes. I get emotional in the sweater I'm wearing. I get emotional on my way into the Dunkin' Donuts. I get emotional on my donut.

When I look at you I say *I am not a white man.*

It has to be said, Harryette, that I'm 28 and stuck in the vortex of being 28

in the age of the internet and liminal spaces. One of my poem's fingers creeps in to my asshole. & everything is there.

There is a pleasure to the body torn to pieces.

Araminta,

Object of my wetness

glistening and protruding wetness

whole like the historically abject

unperform all the abled body syntax

This don't want to cohere
but will anyone be my friend?

Dear Harriet Tubman,

I want to use your body for my own pleasures. In other words, to be historical. In other words, I want to warp your flesh around my subject. In other words, art needs bodies & I believe in ritual. In other words, through history, I am such a slurk. In other words, I sniff your garments & cover myself in the glazed sheath of your human skin. Magical restorations in which poems are the only bodies. In other words, I shimmer the guilt.

Bodies are objects Harriet Tubman and, as such, have more power, in others' words.

Your art withholds information from you, and you'll either have to beg for it, or be forced to try and act on your own. This means that you'll have a greater chance of failure. This form of control makes the art feel superior as they know more than you do.

This may be a woman-on-woman violence

Dear Harriet,

My art's project is to compete with the body

terror it!

But the ugly narrative first, Moses
to have a body is to be sobject

The problem we're dealing with is—

                                        —guh guh guh guh!

I can't gut it out, Harryette, I'm stuck in the gutter.

Something I suppose you know well.

P.S. They called you Moses in the same way I call you Hurryet—we erupt the human line.

THE
SENT
ENCE

Your art controls you by putting you down all the time, in public and in private. They might make offensive jokes about you in public, patronize you, insult you or make rude sounds while you talk.

Dear Ms. Ross,

a internet tells me your skull was cracked as a child
a internet tells me my birthplace
a internet shows me your hard-edged stare repeated hysterically
a internet lists out your many names

there's a pleasure in these violences

when I see these things I feel in a Barbara Kruger way, Harriet

EVERYTHING
ALL
OVER
MY
FACE

this narrative violence that history imposes

you were you

I was I

The thick membrane of this happenstance; I'll put my crack on it.

Harriet,

my clit perks and waves to the sun!

it thinks it to be its own reflection

and it looks up the word ENTITLED

At your memorial, I dangle from your big hand like a metaphor: I'm the slobbery noodle.

The way out of this, Hurryet, is through language but I can't stop narrating, guh, it feels so good.

Your art controls you by bringing up private moments that you might not want to be general knowledge, and turning it around so that you come out as the fool and they come out as the hero.

Dear Moses,

In Art
none of us hero.

There are many versions of me on the internet
and they are all arms!

Have you heard:

What a pair of hips can do
to your historical line.

YOUR ART CONTROLS YOU BY MAKING YOU RESPONSIBLE FOR THEIR BEHAVIOR, AND IN DOING THIS AVOIDS ALL ACCOUNTABILITY. IT WILL BE YOUR FAULT BECAUSE YOU DIDN'T REMIND THEM, OR SET A GOOD EXAMPLE, OR STOP THEM SOON ENOUGH WHEN YOU SAW THEY WERE DOING THE WRONG THING.

Harriet,

Please excuse, I'm trying to arc at the moment

Harryette Mullen,

This is so really hystorical

because when I said I was writing about guns everybody winced
because I forgot to mention they were just my metaphors.

I do believe the poet can act like a terrorist
with a guh guh guh guh!

                                                            fat onto the sentence

it's too safe for whats!

here, I'm really writing about a body, as the landscape, Moses
    and the desire to write about that body
    without all the whats

    I think there I found an art there

That sentence can sustain all this
like a pro

can a body

Moses,

Language is a type-o-trash & I'm uncertain about the concept of nonviolence

as in, these letters are all arms

When I pass by your memorial on my way to Dunkin' Donuts, I get the word sickies. Did you hear me, Harriet, all my lovers have white names? The tail end of the statue is a tangle of roots dragging you down to the earth. On the internet there's a discussion about whether you are facing in the right direction: glazing south to where you came from or facing north to where you are going. The artist said you are supposed to be an object here. "She is not represented as herself, Harriet Tubman," it reads.

I have to say this: Am I a using you.

Your art controls your emotions by using body language and gestures.

These can be—sighing deeply, refusing to look you in the eye, making a big show of crossing their arms with a bored look on their faces, withholding affection, making up fake stories about you and calling it art, pretending to be you and wearing your garments when you have already died.

P.S.

As in, last night I could feel your fingers
open up the asshole, Araminta, and all your ghosts coming out,

(UNDO THIS BODY)

as in, another type of historical error

as in the closing line of this love letter:

> *You are a huge thing/*
> *I can dangle from.*

(POEMS ARE THE ONLY REAL BODIES)

I know for certain
bodies were made to be weaponed
and so my desire was born

Your art controls your time by making you wait
or even by not giving you a direct answer
to your question and replying with a "We'll have to
wait and see."

Experience starts with the guh. I know of you, Conductor, in the way I know myself; the poem is many armed.

I read the following on a school teacher's website: **We are dying to have a Harriet Tubman Day because we should not forget her.**

When you get to the end, you have more sincerity that wants to tickle out, but this body is tried.

Harriet,

This is a poem I did not write:

<u>5 Senses Poem About Harriet Tubman</u>

I am Harriet Tubman. (who)
I was walking on the Underground Railroad. (what)
When I saw a slave trying to get away (who)
At 5:00 in the morning (when)
To get to Canada (where)
For freedom. (what)

By Jonathan and Chris

There's a terror that we will love

too many people in one lifetime

and won't give ourselves to any one

sentence

Dear Mrs. Tubman,

There will come a day when body is an abolition

I can't be sure who I am because she has no way of speaking.

YOUR ART CONTROLS YOU BY DEFINING YOUR REALITY. THEY DISCOUNT YOUR EXPERIENCES AND REPLACE IT WITH THEIR TRUTH AND REALITY WHICH IS ACTUALLY A LIE. FOR EXAMPLE, "THAT'S NOT WHAT HAPPENED," "THAT'S NOT WHAT I SAID," "THAT'S NOT WHAT YOU SAW OR FELT," OR THE BEST ONE OF ALL, "I KNOW YOU BETTER THAN YOU KNOW YOURSELF, HARRIET TUBMAN!"

Amarinta,

The e-pistols are filling you from the inside out. The e-pistols are pouring into the ear hole, the belly button hole, the mouth hole, the pee hole, the eyehole, the butthole, the penis hole, the throat hole, the stink hole, the vein hole, the vagina hole, the nipple hole, the brain hole, the tooth hole, the stomach hole, the face hole, the bone hole. The e-pistols feel the holes from the inside out, until the hole is stuffed and bursting. The sheath of your human skin becomes less and less. It's almost translucent. It's almost glaze.

scenes from the lives of my parents

PATTIE McCARTHY

scenes from the lives of my parents
Pattie McCarthy

5.5 x 4 inches | 28 pages

80# cream cover | natural white interior
carmine translucent flyleaves
pamphlet stitch in natural twine

*scenes from the lives of my parents

she said nice hands
he said I know
(*& this is how my father met my mother & my mother my father*).

*scenes from the lives of my parents

my father shaved his head in order to write
a letter upon his scalp & waited
(for his hair to regrow)—whereupon
he set off for my mother & there shaved
his head again to reveal the message.
this was a period of history that tolerated
a certain lack of urgency.

*scenes from the lives of my parents

            on your way to the mess hall a truck
            will pull up with instructions to take
            you to the dentist—do not ask questions—
            you are not going to the dentist—once
            you've arrived you will take the test
            & find your own way back to base—this
            will be s.o.p.—someone will
            come to take you to the dentist.

*scenes from the lives of my parents

she said
I whas & ys & ever schell
be youwre awne true
bedewomen tyll I die.
[the same wife to her husband]
I rest your loving constant wif tel death

your letters er[4] very short.

he said
what soever I sayd, it was before
your face. I doe not waygh it a straw.
tho shalt see that the clothes I
weare is not borowed; you know
it is not your petticote.

*scenes from the lives of my parents

when presented with the word puzzles
LO _ AL & THR _ _ T men were more
likely to complete the puzzles with neutral
words like LOCAL & THROAT but women
were more likely to choose LOYAL & THREAT.
this breakthrough on the cryptographic
systems was accomplished entirely through
sweat-of-the-brow analysis without
the aid of any captured codebooks.

*scenes from the lives of my parents

shibboleth
(*& this is how my father met my mother & my mother my father*).

*scenes from the lives of my parents

she was coming back from a break—two agents
were standing at her desk—a telegram
had arrived at home—when they reached
her house she saw her father
in the door & she sank to her knees in the front yard.

***scenes from the lives of my parents**

my mother asked the midwife to place
a special stone under her head & give
her a potion—in part of the finger,
toe, & knee-joints of corpses—to ease
her birth pangs (perhaps an alteration of *prong*).
a piece of flexible
material forming the hinge. she was ordered
burned alive. the midwife was also executed.
[I doubt the authorship of this book.]

*scenes from the lives of my parents

they met in the first Voynich study group (1944–46) in which text was transliterated & machined—at least 48,000 characters (or 1663 thirty-character lines). the results & any report of analytic studies have disappeared from the file, if they ever existed. subsequent students have had to repeat, over & over again, all the work of transcription & machine preparation, as if it had never been done by others. as if it had never been.

*scenes from the lives of my parents

she said I love you
he said thank you
she said nie, dziękuję
he said nyet, do svidaniya
(& this is how my father met my mother & my mother my father).

***scenes from the lives of my parents**

she said to whom do you speak this?
he said do you see nothing there?
she said nothing at all; yet all that is I see
he said nor did you nothing hear?
she said no, nothing but ourselves

*scenes from the lives of my parents

Shakespeare makes the closet scene more dramatic by including the appearance of the ghost and the fact that Gertrude cannot see it. the ghost's appearance results in different reactions between Hamlet and Gertrude. the interesting part is that Gertrude cannot see the ghost in account of her being sinful and at this part she feels convinced that Hamlet is mad. Hamlet on the other hand gets confused at why she cannot hear or see the ghost. Shakespeare arouses interest in the audience by making the ghost appear at that particular point. the death of Polonius is also an attempt by Shakespeare to enhance the plot. how to cite this page MLA citation:

"Free Essays–Act 3 Scene 4 of Hamlet." <u>123HelpMe.com</u>. 09 Mar 2012 <http://www.123HelpMe.com/view.asp?id=14579>.

*scenes from the lives of my parents

& boy meets girl—he is a lifeguard—she is reading about the wreck of the *Andrea Doria*—as they say in the army—it's a counter-intelligence lovestory—this information may be given in cipher—this information may be made available on microfiche—tabula recta.

*scenes from the lives of my parents

libel & the matter
now infamously
reckoning
[statistically improbable phrases] 'buttery book'
& bills he could not possibly pay (learn more)

*scenes from the lives of my parents

when I was six I played by myself & drank
powdered milk—& I liked it.

*scenes from the lives of my parents

palimpsest
(& this is how my father met my mother & my mother my father).

*scenes from the lives of my parents

they arrived on the SS Willehad in Fells Point, Baltimore on 4/11/07. the names of their parents are unknown. an unnamed cousin and their children's uncle, also unnamed, purchased their passage. in the 1910 census, the family was living at 721 South Broadway in Baltimore, which appeared to be a large boarding house. she could not speak, read, or write English but all the others could. Johan, now listed as John, registered for the draft listing his d.o.b. as 2/11/77, his citizenship as German Poland. they were working as laborers in a postery and he worked as a laborer in a box factory. in the 1930 census, she was now a widow. all of the sons were single. she still knew no English but all the others did. he died shoveling snow on Palm Sunday, 1942. he drove a yellow cab for many years and had a fatal heart attack when he was robbed by an unknown assailant at the intersection of Fayette and St. Paul Streets. he changed his surname by court order in 1954. here, fill in your father's date of death here.

*scenes from the lives of my parents

curtains swell from windows & fill
the room with naptime yellow light.
which church is ringing the Angelus.
PLEASE DO NOT WRITE IN THIS AREA.

*scenes from the lives of my parents

he was dressed like a smurf (it made the protest
songs less funereal) & she sang
       boiling water   bubbling tar
       smurfs will be frying everywhere
& she held a blank protest sign (now
       it's stock photo) & they
took two steps in place, one step forward, raised
the left leg to one side & then the right to the other
(& this is how my father met my mother & my mother my father).

***scenes from the lives of my parents**

secondly, that the body, taking in the shoulders, makes still
a more oblong figure, crossing that of the head; so that supposing
the woman on her back, the head coming into
the world, is a kind of elipsis [sic] [stet] in a vertical position.
similar rules applied for the wearing of hats or bonnets.
as the mourning progressed, so the hats and bonnets became more
trimmed and fancy, whilst veils became shorter until
they were eventually removed altogether.

*scenes from the lives of my parents

they were old school—messages
sent by shortwave burst transmission or in invisible ink.
they couldn't have been spies, the neighbor said.
look what she did with the hydrangeas.
they last exchanged long glances when they brushed past
each other on the tarmac of Vienna's international airport.

WINDOWBOXING

□   □   □

KIRSTEN KASCHOCK

Windowboxing: A Dance with Saints in Three Acts
Kirsten Kaschock

7 x 7 inches | 44 pages

80# dark gray cover | cream interior
three ivory vellum windows
pamphlet stitch in natural twine

Approximate scale here: 90%

[WINDOWER]

I want a new wife but with all of my old things.

I am tired of the domestic packaging of woman, the imprisoned-cellophane versions. Meatdress.

I will fail to say this correctly.

In some ways, I have already failed; in some ways, I am failing continually.

And this suits me, buttonhole. Pivot and clasp.

The elaboration of woman makes windows grow in enormity, if by enormity what I mean is importance.

The adverb, said to be weak, is viewed as an addendum to, or a subtraction from, thought.

Slyly. Widow-like.

Bereft but not, emboldened by loss. Wise. Liberated from life. Sprung.

Most windows are right-angled, like their houses.

Modeled on the premise that a box is the best shape with which to contort the soul, i.e. book.

Some mini-dresses from the 60s achieved the same lines, and the Volvo.

The illusion of transparency is a problem, as it is with women, vellum.

I like to think of make-up. Adjustment to mood.

The window is thought of as immaterial—certain things permitted fluidity—the gaze and light, but not the head or hand.

Windows are what make domesticity seem picturesque, in that windows make sculpture into painting. Like said Hegel.

History flattens. She can see out.

She could move through doors and into a car, but then store, catastrophe, park, gym, restaurant-with-bar, waiting room, hotel lobby, book, brick, suffocate, twelve-step, home.

Windows can be effectively cleaned with vinegar and newsprint. You want to remember newsprint.

The hand smelling of a kind of vain poverty, of human interest.

Window—deathtrap for a next bird or birdhead.

Thinking open.

[WINDOWØMEN]

I can't do my heart today, fuss till it's lacy, coral, a century or more of microscopic animals.

The men I am are plural and all thumbnails, larger and quicker than that, but clumsy. Overlaid, they palimpsest into substance.

The men I am are wilders—btw, wrong prosecution, a satisfying lying.

In the pack, they slap the bitch down. It is like a whisper. She stays down.

I shrivel when they touch the border of me—when I touch the border of me, I get unvivid and a harder called brittle, intelligent, not-young. The ocean fails. Wombs fail.

The men I am are violent or they are not.

Illicitly got confession. Et tu?

I have never bothered to go fathom-by-fathom underneath. I am more afraid of what I might one day do. Fail to do or say accurately. A bad renovation, the bones unhidden, reef a graveyard, the body drunk up, loved at arms' length (fathom of rope, leash, a good stretch to hang by).

The car, assassination, dishwasher, low-cut: all my fault. Ahem.

[WINDOWNER]

You would have my explosions be localized and armed against themselves.

You would prefer I not discuss "men" or "women." The genres.

It would be better to prevent the spread of the insurgency.

I should not place a woman in a house, done to death—a veranda? Deck.

The way my bombs work is that I set them beside my heart, and although I fly apart and out, flesh of me meeting flesh of the other dead I've made, still I am whole and focused.

My heart, once muscle, now a rapture, now remains.

To contain me, you must rewrite the previous century and go forward in horror from there. As if it were not horror to begin with. You must Whitman.

If I named her field, instead of she, I might have a philosophy, or a beard.

I might be, say, a nurse in the war. More acceptable.

Less shrapnel.

[DANCELLULAR]

This choreography: deaddreams. I make it.

A smoky stage, two dancers trip as if hitting glass. Bird-mimes.

To be watched—a microscopia.

Trapped in waterdrop, underslide. Only fixing eyes to avoid and entertain.

Naked-as-all-get-out, they try to flash each other through dry ice: a game they can't win. It is all very panoptic.

Further revelation becomes gratuitous. Lapdance lazuli.

They do it anyway—the angry stripdown to their DNA. The denaturing.

Skivvious. The smoke makes me sick. Applause, and I bring them flowers called *merde*. They are by this time ooze.

It is hard to remember what comes first.

Aftermath?

I think it a tidier business through a proscenium.

[WINDOORS]

This one has trees outside it.

To be accurate, they all have trees outside them somewhere.

I can see these: a white mulberry, a maple.

In mid-June the postage-stamp yard is a swamp of alcohol, the fruit shedding or shat by birds beneath the lush cover.

A dark and small yard, where nature is still about its own decay, happily.

Satyrically. Big deck.

The windows on the other side of the house look at other windows, but this is not a conversation—this is a subway.

The street rivers between, floating cars carrying other windows.

The city is also about its own decay, and the poorer kids at the neighborhood pool are turned away for not having legitimate bathing suits.

Nothing private is natural.

She has had her shirt blown up by the wind.

She has held her shirt up, exposing her nipples, covering her brown, her summer face.

Mistakenly supposing this will make her nakedness private, but her face is not really on the table.

She is six.

[SAINTHREE]

The third ever saint lived that life at an address. I did: I wrote a paper. It's possible to mapquest it, street view. Stuffed animals in front of the boarded door. Black-and-whites: a zebra, dalmation, two pandas. I google her name to register new intercessions—Girl in Alabama Regains Sea Legs. Coma Victim Wakes. Infertile Couple Conceives. (That last miracle, revoked . . . because of blood type.) Into plaster, a scratched "forgiv." She was six. She's lived—it's called living—at least double that. In the nursing home, she walks with a walker, ever nodding, ever greeting the never-leaving. Home now. She does not like speech, which hurts, but to be walking, slow, as not to hurt. Orderlies call her Poke. Because of the slow. Because of Little Golden Books (the binding). Small face behind a basement grate—eyes of passersby, neighbors blind. Poke. Photographs of after show a sour mattress. Ropes. Toy of dark-and-lighter shreds. A once-penguin, maybe. Just. No flight to it at all.

[WINDORMANT]

I never used to be able to keep things alive, cacti. Jade. I can keep them going now, but at what expense?

I can take   m o r e   a hormone so my unborn daughter will one day push strollers without   l i k e   rancor. There is a hormone for that.
A hormone   f e a r   I take opens my bronchi despite badly planned landscaping: all flowers, no fruit.

Corticosteroids turn me unhappy. But a breathing unhappy.

All the breathing unhappies, forgetting that austerity is a sort of pleasure, except those who have embraced austerity because superiority is an even clearer, cleaner sort of pleasure. Vinegar.

Comfort is overrated. Bliss, a sister's word for drug use.   m o r e / l i k e / f e a r

A nun's.

The pachysandra in the yard—a gift from a dead woman. It is supposed to make me happy but I am only more afraid it will die. The older I get.

I want to own this living stuff, this desire to wrench shit out of the earth.

The truth is something more like fear than it is like April.

[WINDEED]

When I am not writing I am living.

When I am writing I am not living as clearly, as close to the surface of my beige, my negligible skin, but I feel that I am.

Writing—skin itself—is that kind of drug.

[WINNUENDO]

Touch me in the morning, see if I will respond, rise up like a tired plant given water.

I bet I fucking lotus will.

Sudden shifts to sex are confusing until I am reminded, I am human.

The term nookie came into English use in 1928. A nook is a perfect place to put a thing.

In this way, I am cupboard and penis a knick-knack. And nookie/nooky heteronormative. Sex is not heteronormative.

Perhaps nookie is from *neuken* meaning to fuck or punch. So, heteronormative.

We are lost.

Two women on the web were fighting about whether they experienced themselves fundamentally as humans or women.

"Experienced themselves."

By starting that sentence *two women* perhaps I indicated something.

Indicate: point to, as in—a plant on the deck. Dying. I don't always make it outside to water things. My dead aunt-not-technically-my-aunt would find that tiresome. She chainsmoked I-forget-what-brand.

The one arguing womanhood was actually arguing potential motherhood. This, I thought, was unfair.

(S)he took the position post-birthgiving and with the accompanying amnesia. Possibly (s)he was just as much a humanist prick before.

As the other womb, excuse me—human. Thinking open. Cervix.

Anyway, anus. Fundament meant.

Across the interweb, they should have been simply voices-simple, pre-spidered, drunk up by a reckless anonymity, but were somehow not.

I wonder, sometimes, why the rain can't do it.

I want I think to start to blog as a boy. In the mornings, I wish I were erect and could just go.

That is what I mean.

[WINDOWRIGHT]

Window, like woman, an invention.

Think caves. Invent: to welcome wind. To shun: unwelcome.

Windows are doorways un- to pass through. Illicit entrance, seduction, a tease. Stopped at the waist, sill at the hips.

Except when I was in Paris, the windows opened all the way down to my shins, and this is why it is called a honeymoon.

Josephine Baker adopted ten children. I saw a photo. Voyez la résistance.

Before I was invented in pregnancy I didn't exist.

Third person: a window, a child, POV. The bomb, the bomb, the bomb, the bomb.

The Wright brothers thought their planes would be used for scouting. They did not invent mass destruction, no matter what the papers say. You do remember the papers.

Wilbur and Orville marketed their invention to the military. The American military, the French.

Geometrically speaking, a plane is a horizon—horizontal in all directions.

The earth could not remain flat. Because of puberty: it comes earlier and earlier.

The horizontal line vast but not against god. It was the perpendicular that eluded the brothers. Something falling from the sky not by miscalculation but by design.

The window in the bottom of a plane added a new dimension to warfare. As does strapping the bomb to a woman's body, another window. Another way to deliver.

Wright angle. The flying machines began to let the killing drop from where god was.

Now—from nowhere or just north of Vegas—drones do this.

[CELLARDANCE]

I made a dance about torture. I choreographed it.

Yep.

A mirror in it for reading all the advertisements. To see, an entrapment.

A body can be a tool for marketing, even past twenty-two, thirty-three even, because the body is unsatisfied.

Torture was in the dance I made represented by stuffed animals and a ball-peen hammer.

They can take it over and over. I asked for volunteers anyway. I taped out squares on the floor.

One volunteer I gave a panda.

Do you know about the memos? I asked them.

But I asked it with bodies which they had never been taught to read. Not for nuance.

The soundtrack was bureaucratic. Bybee.

Also, there are all these children kept in basements, sometimes by their fathers. This was part of the dance. I represented eighteen years without a window. I had a mirror.

Time passed into.

Theaters have no windows because of not wanting light. Flickers of a thing unseen but maybe paying more attention than in the sun, on the beach, all that flesh, advertisements flying over an ocean turning black since dawn.

I can't really understand what dawn is anymore, beyond its relationship to my person.

My left hand, the eastern hand.

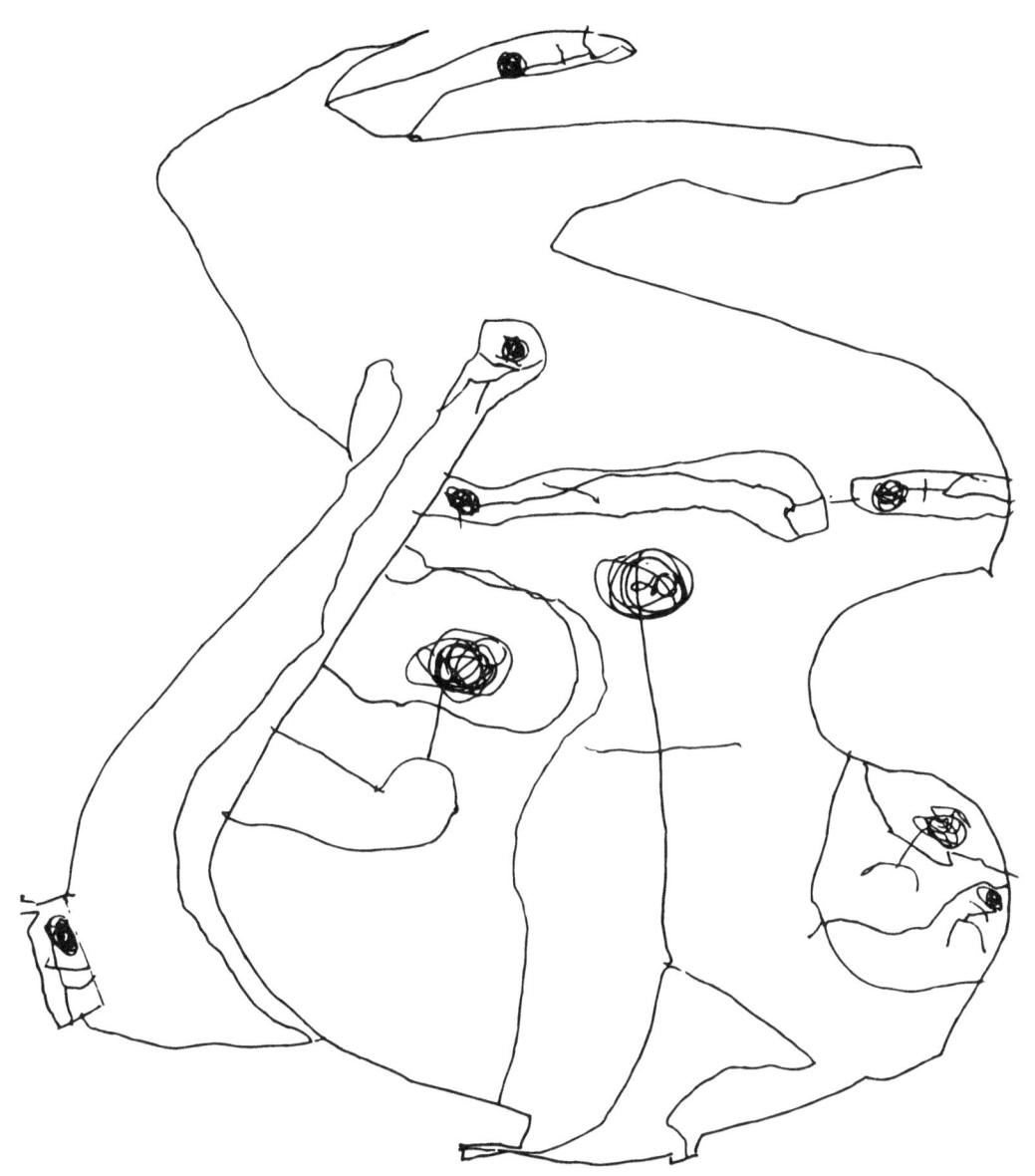

[WINDOWTREATMENT]

If your father or sister molests you, there is a support group.

If you aided them, there is a support group, and serotonin-reuptake-inhibitors to help you with that.

Coffee seems also to be protective against suicide, Alzheimer's, sleep.

For the kind of sleep that keeps family blurry, coffee combined with alcohol is a folk remedy, for four hundred years, prior to which coffee was more localized.

Alcohol is old as family.

To stay together—a buttonhole. Pivot, clasp.

Under the sound of the family, you hear brushstrokes, a percussionist waiting, a painter crying into the palette, thinning the hue, a dancer scuffling, nothing moved.

No thing or one moved.

[WINDOUBTFILLED]

There is sometimes just beyond the window the threat of twins. A doppelgang.

These are not clones. You will not open like a Russian doll. They are more their own than they are yours. Not kind.

Your grandmother had a pair. One died.

Blue leather with leather-covered buttons: depression era shoes—the bomb.

She had red hair before it went white; her name was Kaye.

Yours is black. And one of the twins you are not pregnant with: the bad seed, fifth child. Lessing guessed. Oppenheimer.

A threat of twins is the name for the full complement.

Congregation of sparrows, lion pride, plague of atoms, duck morass—that's not right.

One wants to kill crows: their omenhood viral, priesty.

A specimen. You pee into a cup and this tells us what exactly? It used to be a rabbit died. We don't kill rabbits for this any more, apparently. Mascara.

The hormone only says yes or says no.

Not yes, yes. Not indeed. Not prepare yourself. Not now you are a host.

Not Hiroshima.

On the afternoon talk show the woman behind the curtain admitted to birth at fourteen, marriage at nine. Pay no attention.

On the other channel, the evening news is a fire.

Hoarders have died in their ranchhouse, unable to make it past the newspapers. You remember newspapers. And the name of the second city?

There is no place like ovaries. Nope.

They are also the bomb. And their slow-motion detonation: child.

Possibly child-child—your own death in mimeo. Tsunami.

[CROWDEADANCE]

Three dancers.   Hands weaving.   A smaller flash mob.

A black bird alights. Tourist. Stilling flutter for a moment. Just.

No flight to it at all.

There are fingers. They shred the bird.

Mouths—black also—devour it. Where, I wonder, is *to interpret*?

Also—

By what hands, down what throats, through what systems, moves what art?

[WINDOWNFALL]

Work by rule. Rhyme. Or do not. If I start running here, I fall, but only off the edge of the table or through the bottom of a tree like an Alice.

By root I may find the way under.

Windowless, roots are blind. Unless you consider water a kind of sight. Thirst and gaze are related, I give you. And a tilt from the flask of drink-me.

I'd give you pretty much whatever you asked for and I wouldn't serve myself first.

Pretty much from my mother that is how I learned to be a mother, by which I mean woman, she meant.

I believe woman has been defined variously.

Before I was mother, I defined myself as human. My mother knew I was no such thing.

But an animal would not starve itself, though deprivation is a sort of pleasure. Superior, in the way air can be superior. High above us, air is—for an example—thinner.

Water I learned to love early on. Its prolonging. A tree given water can manufacture air high up in its branches.

The roots of film are flickers, nickelodeons, Muybridge. How often do we ask now what happens between cells, what transpires?

We believe in river. Time is continuous.

We can breathe across the frames, between windows, behind walls, we are sure of it. But we are deprived.

I fill the rabbit holes at the base of the tree, the blankety-blanks, learn to serve first.

What is sill other than sideboard, slender hand outstretched and outstretched in offer of daylight, book, dying plant?

An apple, another book. The deadbird outside, on the deck. Its neck broken. The window did it. Or maybe it was Dinah.

I am like a root. I dig in. Don't see.

[ASKEDANCERED]

I made a piece about architecture. I choreographed it.

The dancer stood in front of a slide show.

Her slide showing.

As if she were a puppet, she was flung about the stage, as if she were the puppetmaster. She flung herself.

Her hands opened like a book. Her hands closed down in black prayer, in burqa. And this is where the audience was supposed to understand something.

I am not supposed to place a dancer on a stage, done to death—a cave? The street.

In November weather, she walked a slow walk on concrete.

City. Few cared to stop/stopped to care. *No window into this*—they might say that. Or, nothing private is natural.

Brought back onto stage, she felt it was less, the stage, than the elements.

The elements are real, she said, feelable—my feet got numb.

Dancers are not supposed to speak.

The stage is utopian: silence, like handguns, an equalizer. She looked at me: between us, a terrible shame.

I flung her about a bit more.

[SAINTWO]

Will my own children be available to carry the dead? I wonder. Will my own children be available

A boy. A boy. A boy. One crashes. One arts. One clowns. So far from me, I am sad like a sad clown. I read from the life of the second ever saint. They request this—the me reading. Each night a new horror brought to bed, a new dragon to slay upon each pillow. This is our warmth. Saint Szabo, I tell them, a tailor not a knight, slowed down to a speed so incremental, every alteration he made shortened the hemline of a god. They are not immediately convinced. I say—like a glacier. *Glacier?* they ask. Eventually (I read this online . . . you may want to remember online), the Arctic Circle becomes an economic powerhouse. Once ice is water, permafrost goes also and ravage is the likeliest invitation. We decide to move. I adjust the blanket. When Saint Szabo died, I relate, he was carried in his chair out to the cemetery. Will my own children be available to carry the dead? I wonder. I wonder—how far? Sleeping children should not be organized by their mother's dreams. Saint Szabo is a lesson to them. A knight is a falling. Except for the one who grinds his teeth, mine are making sucking sounds.

[WINDONEWITH]

Beyond this frame an empty prison. Preserved.

A ruin display.

The mirror and I are becoming friends. We have coffee over the idea *penitentiary*. I cannot stabilize my age.

An incarceration released of inmate. *Haunting* is the root of *poem*.

Absolute solitary was piloted as a charitable rehabilitative practice: hooded heads, eating in isolation, force of silence.

Individual postage-stamp exercise yards. Statistically relevant suicides.

Swollen city, overcrowding, middle-class neighborhood, stench (heating and sewage conduits side-by-side—new engineering).

1971. It closes.

Near-feral cats in corridors willed to vine. A caretaker with bowls of cream.

Do we ever know what we will do to those in our power? Sade. If I seek not to use power, does that leave more power available to its seekers?

A body rots severally inside rusted conundrums.

Exposed root, crumbling plaster, vault, drifting snow, bed frames upended like racks.

Or maybe more like—now like—cellos.

[WINDON'T]

On YouTube, on a woman, flogging. Subtitles read, "It is to be 63 lashes." Someone subtitled this.

She pleads for her mother, there is laughter, a pattern on the back of her robes is like a target.

Someone is telling her to sit down, and to *put your legs out*.

She seeks refuge against a car. The dirt is bright.

Dance teaches what scant thing video has to tell me. Of moments. Of movement. Of the suppression of movement.

I do not know what the gap is between video and other realities.

I may have been pregnant once. Three times. The woman, she may have been an adulterer. A lesbian. An intellectual. I don't see.

I worry about my own offense. Scuffling in the bright dirt.

Butterfly effect—chaos is a theory. I agree we should worry, Wilde. I agree we cannot, Assange. The whips stir air I will feel some day.

And the air I stir?

I agree. I digress, I concur, I reject.

Am I, Mother, *animal*?

Of course—I am.

[ABANDANCE]

I cannot help it: wanting massacre.

A solo. Bluesything.

So. I put a dancer in the dirty street, head down between trumpeted legs.

Never mind it's me. For tone color—I have her hone, selve.

She downs herself over and over, more insistently each sound of brass. The same hurts more in performance than in rehearsal. Because of bruise.

Day after day after that. The dance is months, reinjury—a best practice.

In this way her skin acquires spirituality: purple and green tinged with gold. A mummer, a murmur, a Mardi Gras.

Hold your shirt up. I expose her nipples, covering her none-of-us face.

This might make her nakedness provocative—if her face had ever been on the table.

Cashbar, countdown, townwhore, trainwreck.

I toss her some colored nooses, the kind of rosary that comes off the back of a truck. Mosquito-spray-prayer.

I paint her with horns and beads, a single strand of feminism.

Skimpy fiction unfits her, nymph-blatant. Color her martyr and I am the world.

Choreo-hater. Stig mater.

[WINDOWAKING]

The window is a bed.

This choreography when I cannot sleep: a sleeping partner, an unsleeping partner, a book by the moon by the window.

In Italy—a family, half of whom at a certain age cease to sleep. Nine months later, these die. It is a pregnancy, a whisper. A waltz.

The pas de deux at the Guggenheim? Lessons in partnering a corpse.

Books? Same.

The dance is done with masks and torches in our very window. In the morning I am tired, and continue. One (two, three) . . .

The plot of *Giselle* (in both Rhineland and Creole versions) has a dead ballerina keeping her betrayer alive through the night. He will not die. This is the story—she loves him.

She does not let him sleep.

Last night, another fire on the news. Seven children died while a three-year-old went to fetch her mother from the barn. Father in his truck.

Fire likes a bed. A plot.

Our dance I do in a room next to a room steeped in children. No tragedy.

The Italian family, theirs a prion disease, a smoky veil over their lives, the folding of proteins into eventual fatality, a book.

Centuries ago their sleeplessness ended in townspeople and torches, now it is a room with ropes.

Ends tied to beds reflect a tendency to hurt the self, others: the narrative arc of a curse.

Giselle's mad scene ends only Act 1. Because there is more (two, three) . . .

A mother. A father. A toddler who will or will not grow into the chapters of her waking life, mask over a mask over the other one.

Is this the story—they live?

[WINDOWALK]

I ask them, these people who will not define themselves variously, I ask them what it is like.

One arts, one clowns.

The one-who-crashes tries, saying—it is like being a fast car.

And all I can think of at that moment is *brick wall*. And then I think, *I am thinking of a brick wall.*

We are lost.

We sometimes walk beside a canal floating plastic bottles on the way to water-ice.

The decay, the layers of lead paint off buildings of brick, released into the air at dusk, at dawn, towards all left-handed thoughts—this is lovely.

Commensurate with my mortality, the façades are like the recent fragility of the skin on my throat. This is also lovely.

Lately, I have been touching my own neck with the backs of my fingers, as a lover might.

Where does one find such a lover? I am beginning to wonder.

I buy them water-ice in waxed cups. One vanilla, one root beer, one cherry.

Walking back along the canal, we palm the plastic bottles, shoot them into green mesh trash cans. We are fast cars, swerving back and forth along the towpath, retrieving death, delaying it.

I am beginning. I wonder, *Can what is not enough—be?*

In a jar of fog at the Mütter, the heart's remains begin to split and flake. So many abandoned storefronts in Philadelphia. So much skin.

[SAINTACTONE]

A window was offered to the least among them. On its sill a book. More a pamphlet: autobiography of the first ever saint. The self-hagiography read from during her beatification. Sit here at the window. Read how St. Ipolyta chained the baby sea turtles to her sides, how she encouraged them to drag her bit-by-bit to the ocean. Please remember ocean. Read of their failure, the lolling of their fingerling heads into the hot sand. Read of her disgrace, remorse, redemption. On the sill, perch to discover how she came to know that two dozen infant turtles were a sign. Read how she wore them as they rotted to rosary. How the fishy stench she covered with constant lemon. How she avoided all clatter of desiccated shells. It was her penance: slowest possible motion. Wiles of micro-movement. The turtles mattered less. The stapled manuscript explains—her belief was the miracle: the heart she proved. Tremendously slow-beating also. It was a task ascertaining her death, as she kept startling the grievous with sighs. Here is an apple. Leave the core just there beside the window. And the tract. Time is a quality of movement. Every thing will be taken care of.

> Mine by fault and final ordination. I remember the pulse of eggs in the late sun, their vital push. Beaky mouths rending what was hard—only then to strive impossibly toward surf. To have them take me, also impossibly, with them, to quarter me, to make me chum: this is why I caught them. But first, I needed myself. With fishhooks I pierced the sides of an emaciated body like a seam. I bound hooks to chain, chain to other hooks, and these I sent into the brave fumblers. They'd no shoulders for yoking but only divots of regret where I punctured what was not yet hard . . . It was then they began their dyings—tiny, errant tugs along my bloodied edges. My unspreading form was their first, last constellation: I lay before their fading as before God now—goliath of fastening.

[DANCESTRAL]

I make it this way: I put a glacier on the stage.

It melts.

There are compensations. For example, an audience drowns.

Doing nothing is its own war.

I choreograph saints by initiating total paralysis. It's not the fire, it's the being tied to.

A boy without a brain kisses a girl without a heart. She returns it. It's what empty drums do—the ocean turning black since dawn.

A girl without a heart kisses a girl without a heart. On the internet. The room heats up. The world is heating up. The suicides happen somewhere else. They happen here but don't matter. The desert comes quick. The stage, lit by alcohol, burns. Home is an excavation. Beneath coffins of dust and greasepaint, she is all skin. She can scroll through herself. Remember scrolls.

Windows reflect her in ghost.

Murdered is the most common means by which to become holy.

She watches flickers, knows what happens once Loie Fuller has waved her tinted sleeves. After Isadora nakedly graces the graces. Post Bojangles kicking and climbing, unclimbing and kicking, the pointless stairs.

A window is a painting someone has forgotten to put the painting in.

Between cells, there is neither osmosis nor love note nor hatch for escape.

To peer is not to pass.

Because defenestration is a ladies' game—

anyone can play.

Packing
Hailey Higdon

5.5 x 8.5 inches | 24 pages

recycled cardboard cover | various weights
natural white interior
saddle stapled

Approximate scale here: 75%

It's Dark or Whatever You Call It

How long can I stay

stuck they say—we are

all entirely undiscerning

sit back, and enjoy that other people are

creeping in too, just asking questions

allows them to fasten around your life.

A gift is an example of a hierarchy, see elegance

for another   of how we broaden over,

ourselves over others, instead of

fixing those bad links like a nook is

virtually the same as a book, but a book

is considered the broken form because it comes

in what   is considered by some

to be a finite expression, 3 men

sit on a wall evenly placed like runners and

I turn around to watch a cop in love

park and 1 man is gone when

I turn back a shift in the ranks as significant as one lightbulb going

out in a long string above the vanity mirror, minor

but not without connection

to the larger

vision, outside outside, the vision or the

dream that everyone is connected to everyone else, don't barf, this is
serious,
which maybe we should call *relationship,* the
binary that allows something to be present, presented, to exist or the continuum
of even one
event occurring after another when we retell the story of it
but actually these things occur upon each other too   *fat*
or was it *compound* interest, the adding of an event as a cushion, suggesting that
the thing that follows is necessary to hospitality, to host the bone.

In the news there is a hoopla about walking horses here, in training
there is something called soring, to raise the knees, make the gait what
they call the Big Lick, and that's funny because it's not like that at all,
it's halting, abusive and it looks like a unique, funny and
animal way of swimming on dry land, only half the horse's body's okay with drowning.

Any Day Bill

any day now
remind me
any day now Bill
I'm gonna get me a house
a good mortgage
when the money comes
you and me Bill

Packed

Would if it is true I've been watching a lot of movies about how we waste—what we get from the earth—all we eat—the holes we dig to feel safe and sleep

the common theme is a menace, all my books are packed

I am looking at the paintings of Joan Mitchell, how something can be your tree and you don't waste it by owning the image of it so

a c-h-o-r-d can create union
a c-o-r-d can create union
a-c-c-o-r-d can create union

together the dirt we eat—led led led into the house, onto the floor by our tracks, we shuffle

I pile things of the same size together, throw away a lot of paper

and sleep the common theme is a menace

a witch a monster Bt corn an early morning if the

wind figures out its ailment I'd be content

crossing the street it's the looking both ways

there are so many little places things sop instead of sit up, but this

is the last of these poems about those places in this city the trash

is in the country too

smooth gliding

across a country road the coke bottle falls off the holler down the holler, holler holler

the sound cooperates with the beauty of the place and the object defies it

as I said, all my books are packed, things are together, in the object sense

Apple Bottoms Etc. When You Are Ready the Conversation Is Waiting

The people in the middle are the bevel

The bridge from top to bottom

Tho usually I am, today I am not referring to the middle class

I am talking about the gray areas of sexuality

I used to believe companionship was necessarily connected to sex, now I'm not so sure

I'm sleeping next to a woman whose hair looks like a wind tunnel in the morning

                                            like WHOOSH! like AH HA!

Bodies come in so many different forms

                                      for instance APPLE BOTTOMS

                                            for instance LEGGY

These small choices like the small addition of a small pollutant to a large river—wrapper, butt, keep us relatively conscious of our position or type—gendered, sexed, top, bottom

We buy our time on credit and by that I mean only that we are quietly suppressing the thought that if we don't pay now we pay more later

I don't know if I believe that or if some people are held responsible for their carelessness in identifying people from objects

There are so many bullies so much defense and so much catastrophe anyway

For instance me:

               on day one of my vacation I was bit by a dog

                       on day two fireworks

                             on day three fireworks

                                   on day four a visit to the ER

                                       on day five an airplane

I have compartmentalized my day into something linear

As if there were a singular definition, something serial and discrete

All our directional abilities to objects become

I have hated or loved

And now there is here

I begin to believe that some people are only capable
of being the crusty bouncers
of friendship, in or out, there is definitely not a reparation
for the sorrow or pain and so much
catastrophe anyway anyway anyway
seems like there are fewer curves
not as many directions available for motif
though TRYING is always a position you can take

Why Not Minot

if given a place to stay
some chips some discipline
the discipline of a situation
it and how it is unfurling in a regulated way
what you're supposed to do and when
does not not follow
like a fallen hat, dead soldier, one of the socks
older doesn't provide any new chances to kick a habit easier
bad habits follow in the idea that we enjoy pain, enjoy suffering, I seek it
try to explain why
how this enjoyment makes me a more motivated person or why
it takes three women
to warm the car and one ice-block to freeze the bed,
one oven to cook it
let's split it, the difference I mean,
that's the way it crumbles
five nickels, a dime, thirty-five cents
and the common denominator thick as a brick, expected
believing that people are good
cookie-wise, I mean

So Many Churches for Sale. Moving? Why Building?

No surprise surveyors make up
work to do   WHO NEEDS THESE

stats cabs to be yellow bricks
red why remember the price
of one thing if the price of that one
thing doesn't change? MARGINS
move longitudinal, felt angry,
felt unjustified, the times you watched
one cut in line in front of you
do they bother you? cause they
bring me to tears and

and that which runs both ways—ownership
to take place or to take your place
to take his place or be taken, take the place of
we annotate the art by the ownership
ownership instead of the framemaker—MAKER
OWNER the recommended viewer the viewer who recommends it to you
puts it in front of your face faces smiling smaces
LOOK HERE the preferred recommendation
for a good time
in this house
is silence—SHUT UP I'm watching the art and

and it goes up up up like a hot air balloon
even when we feel like we're losing
making up the survey to be surveying the land
up up up even if there are not prospects for next year, I mean,
you may disappear and lucky enough I remember alone

When

we count a win

    paint it a color

I bet on the bracket

and I won, I'm always winning

picture that guitar a new color, *Oh brother!*

something different
something different happens
she left
she left the building
she left the bar

make a number two with a loop, *Oh brother!*
you make two arguments out of a sentence

it looks like a good fix but nothing like it

I'm given to gaps and traces

God, I love numbers

I have a scar over places

patchwork, fixing

like a wheelchair acts as legs but is nothing like legs, nothing like it

nothing like my skin looks like, that's a crutch for my skin, a crutch

Oh brother!

this isn't the dialogue
the back and forth I intended
I intended so when does the shit hit the fan?
I start to pay?

bargain all these, for all these good things

/hand/me/silver/platter/
hand me some time

this too is a way
winning, the creation of new skin, more time

my play of the day?

this one on *this* table

I see these things as risks

    —sickness as a risk

        at least I've got my health

   —I say, speaking at risk

      saying

          "like this part, my cheeks"

      saying

          "they're flushed."

Do you know that since you visited I haven't flushed my toilet?

It's the little things that add up.

Talk about winning, the lemon water just sits there controlling itself.

And now *here*, which is also *there*, at the bar, one of my favorites, *Oh brother!*

Maybe I'll go there later?

After I read this poem, I'll go there later, control yourself, *Oh brother!*

It helps to mention we passed a guitar in the trash on the way, we are sitting near the bar, there is basketball on, I have bets on it,

all the fats are here
arms on the bar with beverages,

"Ah good, I don't want any part of it," one says

and

"Elizabeth Taylor died, why didn't I hear about it?"
and then

"I want in on it, all her diamonds."

It's getting late.

Time curls up and we finally notice.

I tried to picture that guitar with some strings on it, the banners with menu items in different colors than what they were—a particularly human brain ability—tokening, right?

Is that how we know who wins?

Isn't that how we determine who is popular?   Knowing

what new things we can imagine they use for legs?   Knowing
what additions they can carry?

I think this time, I'll not sum it up so

/hand/me/silver/platter/now/

like she said, I want in on it, all her diamonds.

The Stone That Produces Milk

the leper in me is forgiving
everyone scouring
getting clean by abrasion, elbow grease

let's shoot for July to untangle our attachments
we've been ignoring our rudder, sending up flares and
waiting to be found instead

in the puddle stopped one wet woman, wear and tear
not on behalf of herself, accidentally, similar to
accidentally it broke, but nobody broke it

I've been meaning to write a story about doctor's orders
how others can compel us
how your friends can go all broken record on you

but doctors, established, all that schooling
one tip and I hop to

let's review:
I clean up my act, use soap
try to find my way and take the hooks out of the holes, dense like Velcro
the wear and tear seems accidental
and I don't fix it myself unless I'm ordered

I've been relearning how to play this Strauss song called "Roses from the South" in preparation for moving home. I think about my mother's knockout roses, my Aunt Kay's knockout roses, all the knockout roses everywhere. They grow so easily. They are always attractive.

back to the idea of polishing, shiny vs. rusty

would if your relationship to the people you loved was like polishing a stone?

something NOT alive, but you relate with—you scrub and you scrub

you wear down or heal nicks, notches

one day when it is smooth, polished

you hold it in your hand for so long it forms there

grooves around your fingers, erodes someplaces

you decide not to let go but to keep it relative to you
you are the actor in the relationship

you love the stone

it stays, only moves or changes in relation to you

when really what I've been polishing is the face on the back of my head

the mirror components

my elbow that bends the other way, my foot that leads from the other side of me

still, I'm moving to Nashville so I wrote this song about forgiveness:

He is a cold cold stone my darling
when things go south
he is a cold cold stone my darling
don't wanna talk it out
he is a cold cold stone my darling
don't let me in and though I
know know know my darling
I try again

Everything Matters

Everybody's got a sticker price mine's a lost glove how
cheap and sad it is to be in love with objects, and let them crowd you, govern

yes I'd love you if you were a sheep, maybe
a machine even—love the sound of you of the machine you
you waking up from sleep

more
better
than what I make

      "blah blah"
again

      "blah blah"

      "bleck"

      "eish"

what a washed out way to clean the slate

you are such a carefully made machine, even tiny parts are so important on you we
test them before we connect them to the rest of you, how diligent, deliberate

same way
I carefully repair tiny holes in emotionally important clothing, darn darn
the sheep you is useful forever, wool, what a thing!

just like how during hard times we use the building for housing, use each, every part,
the high school gym invites a cot convention and Duncan Regan attends in Japan,
brings useful things, canteens, tweezers

the ocean got pushed over to our shore, their shore, barnacles drab, drag, starfish
unstuck and then splat to a new spot, sponge bob says ouch

too cute?—cure me, the superhighway of super sexy super shit
poetry is everywhere—smog full traffic, dusty wind blows

back to you, say what stays and what goes, what gets
lost and what do you tell to get lost

sheep sheep follow the dark dark into nowhere and them let them be done with you there let them get over your usefulness

how thoughtful, details
how many trees chopped down and then move down the line

how much of a helping did we throw out? (I scavenge aggressively through the trash)

what did we lose?

we lost business, pleasure when the street closed off, repairs repairs

about lifestyles, it takes all kinds, animate sheep or plastic ones, every thing matters

30 Years Happy Birthday Anyway

                                                                                taken in, a new

trait or once   I developed

                ability   only when completely

taken, the birds peck

transient,

                            ya so what

I'm not afraid of being a monster

                            to say, fuck it, I gotta case

of the Mondays   still after all, still

this time, after all

                                      30 years, happy birthday already, oh?

to know what's

                    good fer her, people are never

done

                    pollinating each other

as if the flower alone was not enough,

pay attention, it's possible we don't benefit.

THIS IS WHAT IT IS LIKE TO BE LOVED BY ME

JARED WHITE

*This Is What It Is Like
to Be Loved by Me*
Jared White

4.25 x 9.25 inches | 24 pages

80# denim blue cover
natural white interior
stab binding in natural twine

Approximate scale here: 70%

This is what it is like to be loved by me.
A poem of only observation of you and you observing and you hungry. You sleeping doing an impression of me sleeping. You moving the hand at the wrist. Hinging at the waist. At the elbow. Bending at the shoulder and neck. You hunched and articulated. You with stripey shirt and legs. Bending knees hipward so the fabric bunches because the material has to be preserved. With a biggish buckle. And a natural strand that is yellowy, not willowy, roots in the soil to bicycle over and go bumpety it is okay we can walk up this next hill. I do what you do. A poem of being slightly in front of or behind you. Of bounce in step bespoke. A poem of me sitting up and you lying down. It is October 7. It is difficult to notice too much. New boots. New silly I you say constantly. The dimples little curves I touch you there and the caressed divot makes a tiny hum of breath. Another hum is a song but which song I don't recognize. Songs spoken aren't necessarily poems. Silent hum, silent chew. Peer is always hungry chew. Peer must be edible chew. We can also cross at the crosswalk but why not cross in the tunnel flooded with water only the first part is flooded. You put out your hand and offered me something.

You cupped.

Have you seen? Have you seen

Where are my? Up

This is what it is like to be loved by me
if my breath went down into my stomach and my food went down into my lungs. I chased you for an hour then I sat like a reader reading a book but not an actual reader an actual book. My poem my novel is one sentence long

I hope I hope

and I am surrounded by evidence

and I am an evidence maker

I could read the words in my mouth because the words have words written on them each word inscribed with the word it is and each mouth tattooed mouth color with the word mouth in the language the mouth speaks, not mouth as it might be celestial and expensive but affordable mouth, adequate and obvious and constantly available. Happy character, mouthing ablutions of words read and knowing how unlonely it is to be the same in Philadelphia as in New York.

This is what it is like to be loved by me
in another city where decisions turn into money and Peer is a capitalist. I know I should be angry but the thing is, I'm not angry; I don't even exist! I rewrite, I correct, I forget. What is history in the face of amnesia? The editor in the coliseum chose who would face the beasts next, and wearing what armor. Originally it was the armor of

vanquished enemies. Dying is expensive. Punishment is never satisfied, nor is fear

who wouldn't rather ache less longer

or be happier for a while

or feel more

the subtlest feelings. Anxiety of already, of the potential of the chair to be sat in. Farrah tells me my voice is lower speaking foreign languages.

This is what it is like to be loved by me

writing a poem of not you. Starting to talk beyond conceiving since already I felt so happy at the rhythm catching up. Musical metronome. The length of time of a feeling. Exhilaration has levels. I was excited and it made the car drive excruciating. In the bathroom planning my naked surprise I pivoted.

"Can I pee?"

bladder and prostate

fingers like rain

And the sun over the sea onto my body simultaneously. A molecular reception. Me me-made of very deep skin all the way through. Almost smacking kissing smacking. The bug moment when I jumped, something unexpectedly grazing my hand. And where is your every chicken pox scar and how immediately can I find them?

This is what it is like to be loved by me in a pool on the seam where the shallow end meets the deep end and it is not a very big pool it is a hotel pool that seen from above makes a divot on one side like a heart or a kidney. You did not notice until I pointed it out and then you knew something you had not known previously though soon you would forget and I would forget and only this sentence would remember. And in this sentence you and I would go on remembering and swimming in the pool that is inside the sentence and breathing in the pool underwater looking up at the world above the sentence from which you can look down at the sentence like a heart- or a kidney-shaped pool

without reading

what you have written

and without remembering

This is what it is like to be loved by me once the light that cut through the fog has stopped cutting through the fog and now the fog is the fog around which what I see depends on where I stand. Some kind of intuition that I am running out of time, after which the mood I bring to the room will paint the room colors both wonderful and irritating. Like Gertrude Stein's *Stanzas in Meditation* read during a week of grieving, hugging a statue made of ice while wearing many thermal layers, hot in winter, cool in summer, as it is never summer or winter here, only a fog of late spring, early autumn, late spring.

This is what it is like to be loved by me

wait wait, deletions. Lag between entrance and the light on the embarrassing tomato captured at one million frames per second. Theoretical brown shadow made of cave and fury far exceeding both 2012 and 1867 proportions. Lateness. Parallel blocks of identical brownstones. The ribbon ruler. I used to hang a still life in which the unnecessaries obstructed the object. Now I'm only tempted to hang, alone in the house with binoculars, bathtub, and the windows' rattling, escaping from good apocalypse into chintz,

cloud bisected by shade

blue of the moon

Venetian plaster

Throwing pieces of paper into the volcano, the other volcano. Some experience! generating my own internal after-the-fact quake.

This is what it is like to be loved by me
carrying around a tiny container of nutella which I don't even like but you do. What is more important, patience, fortitude or focus? My backpack has fused itself to the sweat on my back, my bicycle groans below me with the weight of children, Peer is sitting in the basket, and no work gets done or at least no work I want to talk about. Some sort of glorious holiday has been announced weekly or even daily and so although the bread we eat is good for cheese but not for sandwiches we picnic, leg over leg, and unexpected leg, for no leg is ever expected when a leg is unimaginable.

This is what it is like to be loved by me
total Romeo total Peer. Begun as a comedy it ought to end as one. Affection, particles and filaments making a syntax of making

I kiss a number

into your scalp

and it overgrows with hair

The cult of movies. Wedding the yarn and the needles. I love you because I love everybody but I love you more. It is a competition. There are auditions. The actors portraying us tell us how we look each morning. They study our trash to fill us with hope. What will we do when words are no longer about us as the stars are, liquids that having flowed now bubble. To be astrophysicists or cinematographers, studying the white balance and the red shifts. How I long for such positions.

This is what it is like to be loved by me
as Rimbaud said—You's another. You's with empty open mouth pocked near splitting. You's neck. You's poem of the skin not being totally attached to the ribs and the music of that object placed object over object, A over B, B over C, and so on through the alphabet like a piano under a blanket turning out to be unlocked. Like a salt flat in Utah but only if something useful could be buried underneath a salt flat. There used to be an ocean there but that was on top. Have you learned how to sail? Once you get seasick it never lets up. Sleep it off? Time's own baptism—Sailboats in the desert—Utah in Africa—Africa in the car—What does the radio play this time? A poem of what used to be on the radio and what hasn't yet been on the radio

You's you

You's another you

You's another another

This is what it is like to be loved by me
translated from grammar into arithmetic and agriculture. But the close people are good people. Are an excuse for incomprehension but also sideways. As if you could

instead work some click click machine. Good is what's alive. Public policy! I told you how plants work and how they need you to stop listening. Then I thought about all the things I think about. But it scares me. The possibility of sideways. My greenness becoming sleepy. Do you hear yourself?

The animal forgot—

some kinds of trees

are also flowers.

What was it like to do the numbers? Gelatin. A red handbag. Foliage without roots, derangement of the light punctuated by coupledom. Is Peer remote asleep? Explaining some other factor in telling versus sleeping regret regrets. Sleep for a week. And then the grain. Most plants are vegetarian.

This is what it is like to be loved by me
in a dark forest midway though my life. The road to the place may or may not be the road through the place. In the birches the branches make a net to fall up into and there is a hole in the bark of the tree a hole that goes straight through through which I can hear you breathing. How do you always do it! You only move your legs into legholes arms into armholes headholes

breastholes

boneholes

holeholes

And meanwhile I snag in the hole in the tree. Being with you is a trust. What the bed said. What the head said. What the cinematographer said. Welcome to the beehive. Welcome, Peer. I came to a desert without a horizon at noon but at sunset you could see clear to the other side. Gulliver tied down by dental floss. Winnie-the-Pooh stuck his I love you in his I love you I love you!

This is what it is like to be loved by me
in the periphery, everywhere your eye is, isn't. I am watching you sleep as I write so you should be sleeping as you read. What is written in the dark should be read in the dark but will be read by necessity in the light. Being away is a time-based ritual like gardening or sex. On the walkway to the house in which I grew up the hidden key was concealed inside a plastic shell painted to look like a rock but that bore no resemblance to the rocks that had been placed around it for camouflage. Another key hung on a shoelace behind the tools in the unlocked garage and was always covered in cobwebs. Break a window and you're in

Even though I know no one is there

I look out of the windows

expecting nothing

Paintings of landscapes, objects and portraits are equally compelling, but photographs of people are always better.

This is what it is like to be loved by me

on the edge of the ocean or in the middle of the ocean, below decks, the rocking action interrupting the pendulum swing every time. Sitting is a detriment but when you stand up you don't have a lap anymore and I want one.

This is what it is like to be loved by me

question mark

Is this what it is like to be loved by me?

that is a different question

what is it like?

I have watched you while you are sleeping so I know something about you that you don't know about yourself. What do you know? Do you know much? Do you know some? Do you know anything? Do you know if there is anything that can be known? Do you know nothing? Do you know how much nothing you know, how much nothing about everything, or nothing about nothing, nothing at all except sometimes something, something like what it is like to know something, like what it is like not to know exactly but to be known about, to be known about by me and by me to be loved?

This is what it is like to be loved by me

Judaism. They moved Poland. They knocked down my elementary school. They rewrote my education. They went overseas. I watched a movie in which everyone was doing a version of something I remember us doing. Would it be a gift to have a lot of values if they were only temporary and the world were permanent. Bright object with its light turned off. Bright light with its object turned on.

This is what it is like to be loved by me

driving over the edge of the corniche and floating in the car fascinated by the slowness of the descent. The flashing somewhere overhead, the sky with its band-aids adhesived iffily to the gridlines. If what it is like is ours and if it is mine

is it yours

what is it like

totally without if

This is what it is like to be loved by me

what it's like to be what it is like. Things I did were scary things ideas. But the poet philosopher does not know how to declare war. Liquid retaining the shape of the jar lip of the jar lip on the lip. OK, can we at least agree on everything? Snow monkeys. Surf monkeys. My next summer's next winter's resolutions. I am upset I didn't know you were upset. Then I move to Japan but only if you are invited.

Your experience of a mirror is not my experience of you my experience of you is better.

This is what it is like to be loved by me
under many ticking clocks, for there are many clocks if even two clocks tick, or two tick louder than a third so that the third's tick is inaudible and small, and the two clocks' ticks tick not at the same time all of the time necessarily. The big gears move slowly and their turn is almost imperceptible and yet they drag forward

a machinery of tiny gears

which spin so fast the teeth blend together

into a perfect circle.

and we dance to the tick tick-ticking, or we don't dance. But if we are not dancing as the ticks tick, if we have chosen not to, what dance is the dance we aren't dancing?

This is what it is like to be loved by me
on the run. I run for health not for cover. I run for my office. I run for implements. I run towards and away from. I run a string across the hypotenuse. I run in footprints. I run from surf. I run stopped. I run my finger across your nipples. I run down my chin dripping onto the floor. I run with pants around my ankles. I run on food, I run on batteries, I run on sentences. I run to run, and when I

don't say something and when you don't say something it is because we are running side by side out of breath.

This is what it is like to be loved by me

by my beard hairs, which are longer than usual, growing more out than down, like a Russian prince. I have decided not to shave my beard until I finish *War and Peace* and then I will not shave it until I read *Anna Karenina* and then *The Brothers Karamazov* and then I will shave and my cheeks will be raw and loving. The skin will have skin all over it up to the very edge of my mouth while the filaments of shaven beard hair will be hairy in the sink

Kings!

Princes!

and the single subject they share

down first on one kneecap and then the other, totally promiscuous, demanding health as counted in omissions, commissions, inputs, outputs, repetitions. When you can't lift ten pounds. Some minutes are longer than others, like the feeling of looking at an object at the edge of the distance where the object becomes impossible to distinguish. To hover at that horizon, extended further yet by eyeglasses, where the terrible differences between nearly identical things fade away and all things, scrawled over and over their surfaces with words so small they can never be read even with the tiniest eyes reading through the tiniest eyeglasses, mere instances superimposed over each other so behind it, there it is again, eye, beard, mouth, beard, eye.

This is what it is like to be loved by me
asking a question that is supposed to be answered with silence, and receiving instead pure truth, wet shirt, limp in the chair my rivets have scratched. Where I leave my residue, you pass your finger, sometimes in judgment, sometimes merely in recognition. There is an area on you where your moles make a perfect isosceles triangle now find it. This is what is I am. This is where is I am. This is who is who.

This is what it is like to be loved by me
amoeba prokaryote goo in a stew of organic compounds. I'll race you back. In the swim sea in a swim suit you remember to be overwhelmed are you creative can you breathe with the gills you were born with can you do a handstand one-handed can you seduce a thousand molting seals? But those are sea lions. Do it over do it underwater. The salmon relents imagining all that perfect darkness that irrelevant safety. We are too little and adorable to be afraid.

This is what it is like to be loved by me
as daily practice. Peer had to find another profession besides reporting from beyond the grave. Happiness, a form of

memory. A form of detail. The buzz of taking it with you through the passageway into the courtyard, vines grown so thick on one wall they became a bush performing person as lover-mediating chink. Easy as the wind makes waves, but not tides. So I learned. Waves would not carry me home, waves already teemed inside with babies, their bald scalps and grooved teeth and first birthdays. Only the tides of my stealing and being stolen from, my even accounts balances in the red book and the red-and-white book. Inside the message a curse from the future: this is what will be. The word unlocked the pyramid before the door fell off its hinges and Peer inside did not even look up at his desk from his work, the work of loving, of making making possible.

This is what it is like to be loved by me

as best as I can tell based on what it has been like to be loved by me previously. The leftover yes on me still a little glimmer. I was the mother of an animal. I carried her to maturity, in the itch. I was the father, I met her later after much preparation. How easy and how terrifying it was, like the portrait of the cardinal and his glasses. Flowers in the ears and the nostrils. History is. Making what works for me work for you. By stealing these affectives

repeat

take it home

do more later

You know my secret. Smile in the dirt. Fingers at the end of a foot. Patience. I ought to make a body out of you. Continuance of termination. By narrating my exploits. A poetry of boundaries. A poetry of pottery, of earthenware jars and Ming vases and lumps of clay from the cliffs I swam under, grazing my feet on the rocks covered with mussel shells.

This is what it is like to be loved by me

I say as the spotlight I shine in the mirror illuminates myself. We told each other how much we owed each other and that we would pay each other back once we were paid back each in turn and then we went off to them to monetize the debts. Like a dictionary is a relationship. They have none. You have your intervals but they have other geometries. Being a sector of a circle. Being a corner of a sphere. Against the spirit of such names, the first, middle and last, only in the ignorance of sentences can there be safety. *The Last Tycoon*. I frighten looking at handiwork, one handyman to another. The red hand of everybody who figured it out. The blue hand of disinterested friendship. A gap in agape. Agreement ends the conversation.

This is what it is like to be loved by me

in the Odyssey when most of the time in the epic is spent safe on the island of Calypso, having a lot of sex, wherever the island is, and everywhere is the island. Sex-style sex, going from rhythmical to metrical. Then calm of concrete. Calm of asbestos. Spray calm consolation. My moustache gets too long before my beard does. Fat ass of a god. Everyone is neurotic, everyone is eventually dead. We don't know you but we will, ancestors, patrons, pets, brides, gentlemen, carpenters, sailors.

modem

beeping on the sailboat:

map of the eye of the hurricane

All possible pleasures. Navel, tree scar rock hole aluminum music. Miró and Ibsen in a tug of war over you.

This is what it is like to be loved by me

on the Trans-Siberian Railway, which takes six days to travel from Moscow to Vladivostok. There is always somewhere we have never been but what it is like to be loved by me there already exists. Inside scribbly circles on parchment, a marble. Woodedness of our woody material. And it ends as a contrast. Holy icon from Constantinople, counting one two three four until it became too blurry to signify. Thumb over thumb, wrist or shoulder. Everywhere, fingers of new. Fingers of not for awhile. Fingers of again and again. We have learned the game so now we can change the rules.

This is what it is like to be loved by me

again. Everything happens twice. The army gives back Mexico again. The discovery of radium is once again announced. The Indian summer is again Indian. The rewriting is rewritten. Imagine your arm. Now imagine your arm without your arm. Now imagine imagining. In the car with the engine off I steer the steering wheel. I practice I one-handed I diddle practice. Screw activities! Screw events! Seriously, screw art! I am from New York City and that's where we're from too.

This is what it is like to be loved by me
danger danger every itch feels reasonable. Like which knight am I in tin, aluminum, bronze, steel, titanium. More people die in car accidents more frequently than in any scenario that scares us. From hot rocks come metals the ground threw up the opposite of puke. Of animal and/or vegetable and/or plastic. Good for incorporation. Good for riding horses. Good for the big bend the big band.

Me:

You:

Me:

You. Are there mountains in Massachusetts? Are there mountains in the Berkshire mountains? If we see a horse you say zip one point zip two zip zip more than three zap ten points zap like a defibrillator. Wake up, happy me-man! Wordsworth: Emotion in a car recollected in tranquility in a car in the mountains. That was clunky that came later I married a woman I passed in a stable. I still can't canter. Cantorian infinities of different infinite sizes. Dardar. King Arthurs sleeping under a hill next to sleeping horses, and motorcycles.

This is what it is like to be loved by me

thising and ising and whating and inging. Here traveling up the valley we know what it's like to be inside houses and we will be, plant growing in the window box, hope of a sibling to sible, a morning to morn, a king to k. Morning of the morning, it is morning you are morninging but what do you do with her in the meantime? Do you want to wake up early enough to make the morning?

It is afternoon

all afternoon

and evening

People talk as if in this eternity all things are possible. But the second showing is more exact. The catalepsy travels up my leg once more but this time I know what is happening. White mixed with orange, white mixed with white, unnatural white that does not appear in nature, white that must be cultivated and acknowledged, white that must be chosen from a chart of whites, white of the walls, white of walking into the room. You noticed! How every day you wake up a lion. And what kind of lion. The children go away and come back with their hands full. When I look for them I find only their toys and clothes folded in a corner of the lion's cage. Beware of cages. Beware of danger. Everything might be leaving the morning better than I found it.

This is what it is like to be loved by me
but I'm not me! I'm some wolf! I'm some random wolf at any other instant and a specific wolf, with a discernible personality and a place in the hierarchy. I have a territory and a wolf pack and the likelihood is that our paths will never cross. When my hair rustles it makes a ringing noise the noise bells make when we get married and Abraham circumcises everyone, including the slaves, the servants, and the servants' old fathers, who don't even bother to wear clothes anymore. Those dastardly patriarchs! Now I do dishes and get ready to leave everything like a ghost as if I were never there. In this portrait we whisk it all away. I walk off with the part of your brain that used to remember how to be my stranger, my colleague, my enemy. I know you now I know you. And meanwhile Interloper Peer only wants to ride the wolf, the wolf that looks more like a bear than a dog, the bearwolf he could ride west-to-east into the story. One by one his arithmetic generates maths. If we don't stop him he will reverse-engineer our mysteries. We saved them for when we'd sit down next to each other by the dim light of the fire but now we may have to read them aloud in the friction of the hot morning.

This is what it is like to be loved by me,
chaos and anarchy, freedom and bliss, two versions of the

document I let you read. When they ask you that will be all you can tell them, the first two sentences verbatim perhaps

and you may try not to but you will

for their eyes are round

their mothers are fatherlong

A dog is not a baby, and again more sweetly, the anarchists plant their bombs. They park their cars in parking spots in parking lots in parking garages by parking meters and parking attendants. I root for their bombs and their amateurism. I root in the cheeks, eyes, buttocks. Every sentence should be as long as its ancestor, the judge who underneath robes of black fabric ruffles a coat of downy feathers. Like the dawn, Peer has no mother who breathed a mist not visible but aromatic. But outside the room the scenes go faster, overtaken with patterns of dialogue. All each unwitting participant knew was a bit of the plot which, unfolding in a series of hermetic conspiracies, each one sealed off from the next, grew as a conversation carrying the shock of song. I hum the genius of the earth erupting with memories.

This is what it is like to be loved by me

summed up in a single word that is neither adjective nor adverb used to describe _____. When he was thirsty Peer drank so now when he becomes thirsty he knows he will drink as plants drink both rain and sunlight.

Philanthropy. The surface has totally repelled description, soaked into its marrow. When I broke the code I found the less/more languorous under a spiral staircase. I keep meeting people who know each other and they tell each other how. Like a shirt. Thoughts and pauses to express. Our cooperation was commemorated by an enormous unblinking eye.

Your liking improves me

so I lay on the ball

as it rolled in your direction

Metamorphosis toward improvements. A bird comes in the night and leaves my eyes intact so I can watch it dance masculine and feminine extremes. Control of circumstance. Harmony by another name. In the cold fire, in the ice white flame preserved for eternity and for the time being as I love you on a platform and your laughter and your breath prosthesis and an imported green carpet of permission. We walk down it arm in arm onto the pine needles.

BECCA KLAVER's NONSTOP Pop

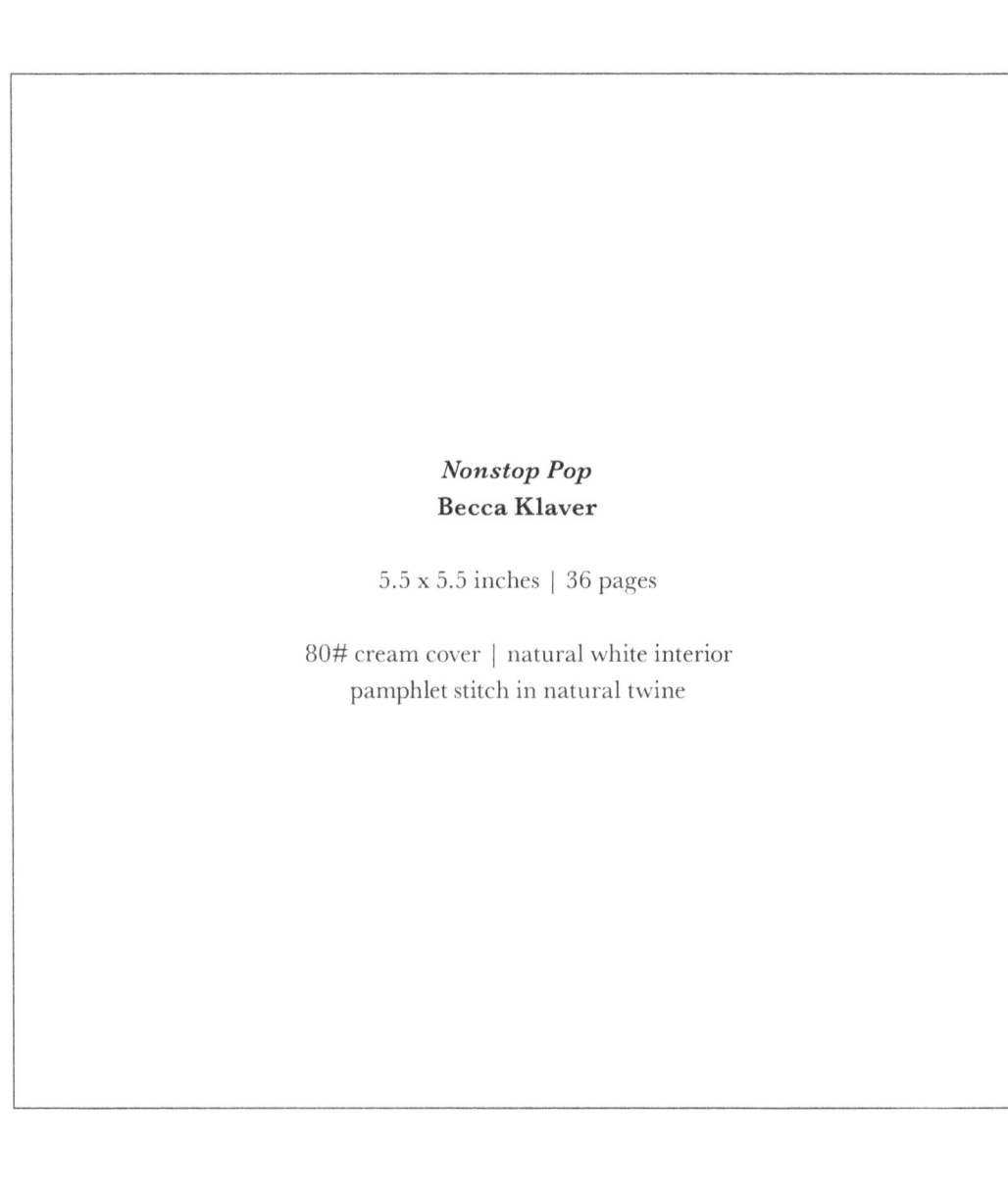

Nonstop Pop
Becca Klaver

5.5 x 5.5 inches | 36 pages

80# cream cover | natural white interior
pamphlet stitch in natural twine

More Lyrics for My Favorite Band

I was clapping for your dance / I was dancing for your clap

I was skooching around in my anger / fainting into a nap

and the girls on the train with their Warhol tote bags
and the girls on the train with their space! gusts
and the girls on the train empire-wasted
and the girls on the train shitfaced-ed!

I was scowling for your benefit / I was benefiting from your scowl

I was facepainting by number / hardsetting my jowl

and the girls on the train go

doo-da-doo / doo-doo da-doo

doo-da-doo / doo-doo da-doo . . . .

On the Night Before TV Goes Digital

PBS is playing *Chattanooga Choo Choo*

ABC is playing the NBA finals (Los Angeles v. Orlando)

On NBC, the greenish light of a hospital room

CBS follows a tan blonde smirky genius

FOX's local news is sponsoring a conversion box giveaway

I am playing a dirge for my friend and tomorrow morning's charges and
    tomorrow morning's pleading

Frasier reruns, *Cosby* reruns, cell phones spandex and storms

You say this is trivial but I take the long view

that was the language we were hearing all night, the poetry of this tall blond guy who spoke like the movies, stopping and starting, making a joke, a kiss

The poetry of television done up in Spanglish and white suits

This is a commercial-free hour

Baseball announcers play themselves

I play myself and Pavement's cover of "The Killing Moon"

Charlie Sheen and his patina

It's April in June, I've got bullion and butter as consolation

Little green flecks float to the surface

My instant / soup and its patina

What can I tell you that will exploit myself and no one else

The man with the red Indian on his cap has won the girl

Oh it's Charlie

Mennnnnnnn

The way to the surface is slow

Morbid, I'm leaving it on all night

A the Beaut

Here we go again, A—

time to lace your bonnet, buckle your galoshes,
glide with me headlong down the Slip 'N Slide—

A, I sewed up the hole in my stretchy teal skirt just for you.

I needle-pricked my finger just for you ess ay

& we became bros.

.
.
.

Hand me the mic. I'd like a word with the rallying forces.

Read book Oprah toldja?

Check.

Can they sell that for you on eBay?

Double-check.

Seen kid-wishes pinned to balloon bouquets
drifting into the lighthouse's gaze over the lake in the fog?

Check again.

.
.
.

In spite of my eyes on the sidewalk
avoiding yours
in spite of small towns avoided
in spite of large swaths of town skirted

we are nightly flying door to door

as a fridge door glows, as an engine stalls

This city's not just a play your mind puts on while you sleep

New, Not Blue

Today the sun is too bright

to know the moon

so I look it up on my calculatorcat

my automated phase display

my e-modulated moon

my interwebbed sky

and the moon is zero percent of full

zero percent of full

and I think

what an optimistic little moon phase

not empty

a bright and shiny moon wrapped in cellophane

not new

give that moon a pretty little bow

zero percent of full

zero percent of full

Direct Address

A cougar was shot dead in your alley this afternoon.
I'm not kidding—a cougar was shot dead in your alley this afternoon.

He went off on a six-minute tangent about *Battleship Potemkin*.
I'm not kidding—he went off on a six-minute tangent about *Battleship Potemkin*.

Famous people are reading poems on TV right now.
I'm not kidding—famous people are reading poems on TV right now.

One time it came to blows over *Das Boot* vs. *Das Boöt*.
I'm not kidding—one time it came to blows over *Das Boot* vs. *Das Boöt*.

It's like the *Yo! MTV Raps* of *Cabaret,* Andy said.
I'm not kidding, Andy said, It's like the *Yo! MTV Raps* of *Cabaret.*

Your mom is my ideal reader.
I'm not kidding! Your mom is my ideal reader.

At the risk of being forward, I'm here on a dare from my friends to ask you out.
I'm not kidding. At the risk of being forward I'm here on a dare from my friends
    to ask you out.

Pavarotti Lip-Synched Last Performance

I love a phony
at the end of his life
in the bitter cold
at the opening ceremony
of the Turin Olympics

Famed Figaro faker
tender tenor
synching

> *Nessun Dorma*
> Let No One Sleep

Every day
I have a lot to say
about What's Real

> *The farther north you get,*
> *the more real the people get*

but most auditors
won't stay silent
and instead react
by way of

> *Okeeeeey*

Hey you
of the eye rolls—

Hey you, mega-concert—
You might postpone five June dates
or cancel eight shows in April but

        I
        will
        not
        let
        you
        sleep

Monday Pizza $9.99

the banner boasts I'm sure Monday
pizza is better than most whatever
the price because it's unexpected
who gets excited about Friday
pizza I guess I do but I'm
excitable or hysterical or some
other word erstwhile tossed at
women who could not sit still

"A Woman Who Could Not"
(YOU fill in the epitaph
don't you LOVE party games)

A. would agree and sometimes
grabs the back of my shirt when I
try to get up from the (fainting) couch

What does he think, that I'm
getting up to "greet suitors" or to
"pace the widow's walk" or because
"my uterus is wandering" only to
"sit back down again"

Until then I will go Frank lunch-
breaking I will go Virginia street-
haunting I will go a-Klavering
I will eat Monday's pizza
for the rest of the week because
I am succored because I am

suckered because the Victorians
couldn't because I can
can you

Schwartzeneggery

She leaves the room and mutters *I'll be back* in a Schwarzeneggery sorta way so it comes out more like *Aisle be bach,* shallow in the throat, and this is just a way around the ordinary, this is just a pump on the pedal to keep rolling along, more awake than before and starcrossedly in love with hurried skirts in doorways, a plate in each hand, a yellow glove, a sponge, a rack, gliding, opening, shutting, championing a lesser-known sculptor. She knows she's not supposed to love it but knows that's why she does, why playing a part with the gust of history at its back evens her out like batter settling, even when she plays it badly. She makes presumptions from the kitchen and she presumes today to be a muscleman.

B®and Loyalty

I was like so . . . Geico

And you were like so . . . Activia

And together we were like so . . . GlaxoSmithKline

In an effort to be so . . . Ann Taylor Loft

We end up so . . . Crocs

And sometimes we're all like so . . . Ambien

When we mean to be so . . . Lemon Pledge Aerosol Spray

Although we're perfectly fine being Pilot G2 Retractable

We'd much prefer to be Crayola Classic Washable

Some days, we must accept, will just be Glad Press'n Seal Plastic Wrap days

I was Kotex Maxi Pads with Leak Lock Medium Flow with reluctance, but still
    I was Kotex Maxi Pads with Leak Lock Medium Flow

Even though you expected things to turn out so Comcast Triple Play

There's a communal relief to being so Verizon Wireless Nationwide Unlimited

In the end I'd just like people to remember me as being as iRobot Roomba 570
    as possible

Foxy

If I've never heard of
The Sexiest Woman in the World

does that mean
I'm past some threshold
of body-consciousness

or does that mean
I'm out of touch

What dude is in charge at
FHM Magazine

who's ever heard of it anyway
and what does it stand for

Image Union

A man introduces the next clip.

I call across the room.

"If you were a gamblin' man
you'd gamble on the one
where the foppish lad
screams berries & cream."

"I'm just in pain
so I'm makin'
faces."

Living the Secret

I am happily celebrating my Secret one-year anniversary this month.

Could The Secret do something for me that's contrary to my friend's wish? Or, could The Secret change my friend's feelings for me?

I decided to "test drive" my power of attraction and started with small things. My first wishes were a cup of coffee and a new pair of shoes, and guess what? Today I have received them!

Just today, an item which I wanted to order online lowered the price by $10 and added more color choices!!

I no longer am picked last, I'm picked first. Everyone notices me and helps me carry my bags to my car and everything. Finding a parking spot is no longer impossible. I get right up front.

One of my co-workers said to me, "You are so lucky, you always win," and I just smiled.

Then I started to use my imagination. I started to tell people that I worked for a FIRM. Sometimes I got really specific if someone asked, and said I work for a Law Firm!!!! I became happy about it . . . . I felt so full of happiness about my dream job!

About a year later my dream came true, she met the man of her dreams! They are married and now I have a loving father and little brother that are a regular American family!

A few weeks ago I got a catalog of chocolate-covered strawberries in the mail.

I am an "in the closet" crazy nut for chocolate-covered strawberries. Every day I looked at the catalog, and thought "yum, yum" (not intending this would be one of the things that would manifest). Saturday morning arrived, and sitting at my door was a big box. Inside there were 12 strawberries and 4 cookies. Just like Jack Canfield, I heard the theme for *The Twilight Zone*. I was so amazed, I cried for 30 minutes (hysterically).

A year later I found The Secret, and realized that I had followed The Secret without even knowing about it! I asked, I believed, and I received!

I then added a picture of Billy Joel to my vision board, as well as writing in my gratitude journal that I already had the tickets and loved the show. . . . A day or two later a woman I work with mentioned that she got tickets to the Billy Joel show on the day of my anniversary. Yesterday as I got out of bed I told myself that today was going to be a great day and how grateful I was for being able to live it. When I got to work this same woman approached me and asked if I feel today is a good day. I replied in the affirmative and she handed me an envelope.

I decided to completely change it around, while adding some mini Secret challenges. I said, "1) I want to just run easy errands at work tomorrow. 2) Before I receive millions from the universe, I want to hear/see something about pandas, and see a hot pink car which will jump out at me."

So far, I'm thinner, my skin is clear, my bank account is bigger, and my love life is shifting.

Loving it!!!

No Country for Young Ladies

A caftan
with extended hard-on
was Oscar.

As plebes fit to any movement—
qualities
from her breastplates tonight:

Why good image,
it's that of swagger
and segmented wit.

I look, camera.
I looked all
together, pregnant, and close-fitting.

Fit breastbone, consumption fit,
darker,
funereal.

They got the
red-dresses-will-eradicate-yr-heart
memo. Right.

Think public:
down
the up premiere escalator.

Insurgent Country

Freeway billboard children
stick antenna tongues out

Air's poised
sound on grass

What praise? sang the
microphone headset

Pious ashen depots—
their ache in tune

to somelips' want
for giant camera rolling

Drunken hills, child actors
dead marbles

& brownbagged
privacy of home-script

America so vast and
usable

Plot Point Two

I love so much to arrive blubbering upon plot point two the part where
the protagonist is driving in the rain or her lover has been unfaithful
or his mother is not really his mother or all three at once   It is then when
I clutch my cherry cola and bite down on the straw and am so grateful

for the Hollywood Formula for Syd Field and those men in black glasses
who sat in back rooms tapping cigars charting the hills and valleys of story
I love to anticipate the sad part 60 minutes in when everything seems
hopeless but really you know the rain is manufactured and the hoary

old man in the garret will get his memory back and reveal that the hero's mom
is really his mom and his best friend's mom too and all along the love
they'd loved had been tucked like a script inside their cells   And when I think how
in life I don't know when plot points will pour down from above

I tug at my hair and gnarl my eyebrows and offer desperate frantic praise
for the staged break-up under the antique lamppost haze   No praise
for flat coke and wrinkled straw and the sicksweet ache my stomach gets
warning me of the bad thing that hasn't come but is coming one of these days

I Was a Water Ballerina

A water ballerina starring in
Marti's Last Stand

A humorous quality to it not because
my father was a big-band member nor

because of my days in the water
pretending to be a contortion artist

but because
girls learn their own layers

A humorous quality to it not because
gum and borax in a heatproof bowl

(I use Pyrex) but because if
Lina Lamont had mixed it with milk

instead of gold, or EVA-Foam
Material instead of with

artists, the girls who play with
artists, the girls who play with

figurines, waterglobes, snow
nods to art in the Chanel show—

my days in the water pretending
to be a contortion artist

would be over. The girls who flashback
for gold, who play with EVA-Foam—

he would never see
my days in the water pretending

he would never see
mother was a water ballerina starring

in *Rich Gold Material*
(10 to 16 August 2003)

not because women are
tutu globes escaping orbit

but because playgirls make
excellent display artists

Less Finesse, More Spank

less *Twin Peaks,* more *Ru Paul's Drag Race*
less velvet, more velour
less Dom Pérignon, more André
less diamond, more zirconia
less UV, more Faux Glow
less sugar, more Splenda
less manchego, more Velveeta
less treadmill, more Skechers Shape-ups
less café, more Facebook
less grass-fed beef, more T.G.I. Friday's potato skins
less pitch, more Auto-Tune
&c.

The Superlatively Derogatory Colloquial Epithet, *Shammy*

You low-down shammies can put a gun in our hands but who is able to take it out?

Make one move, shammy, and I'll blow you away.

Oh, Life's a shammy, Bruce.

So I keep concentrating very hard, helping the pilot fly the 250-passenger shammy.

Eight milk shakes (why had he bought eight of the shammies?).

Where are the harpoons on this shammy?

He said who put this hole in this shammy's head. Who could the murderer of this poor man be.

Ain't that blackshammy beautiful.

I'm one shammy that don't mind dying.

A prudent shammy like me has an IRA account, some short-term T-bills, etc.

Have I got a shammy of a stunt for you!

The Berkeley quartet opened its set jamming and vamping. From then on it was a shammy. . . .

I could turn and run like a shammy and dodge my way back up the hill to safety.

Squeaky-voiced and foul-fuckin'-mouthed as a shammy.

You a bunch of jive shammies.

Leonard Carlo is so upset, he can't even curse properly . . . 'shammy!' he says at last.

Red Arrow Down

Quarterlife bodies tap toes
picture foreign airports at Christmas
imagine Japanese characters for

   connecting flight

tattooed on our tailbones

bitchy reveries
evolutionary tailspins
dream the dream of averages

    sticky bar stool on the eastside
    hatchback for weekend errands

     We are falling off

We think "America"

   and "eye contact"

are the best ways to stay on

The more we get to know you the more
the overlong petticoat of pettiness scratches our ankles
   nips at our heels
      sinks in, fangy

Everyone laughs at our lunchtime propositions

and begs instead for travelogues
Choose-your-own-imagination-replacement

NO VACANCY

IMPLIES A FULLNESS

sputters neon in passing

Boho Wrapper

this urban outfitters
monogrammed candle
is inciting a vague sense
memory nostalgia is
flexible and cheap
you can buy it all over
america though i'd
recommend a college
town there is nowhere
to sit and relax anymore
just sandwich shops
full of manufactured
vintagey gimcracks
and a chorus of sassy
voices hollering
through the fonts of
signs that want you
to believe that jimmy
is a downhome lad
like you i am neither
a lad nor at home
there is nowhere
to while away an
afternoon any longer
and there's nothing
metonymic about
saying bank of america
took it all away nothing
hip or glossy about this

tragedy people not
being able to relax is
as real as problems get
meanwhile across town
you keep open the last café
and thank you and
bless you though your
fingertips are calloused
and you cannot sit down

Definition of Destruction

(b.) Along with its pal, Creation.
(ca.) The Big Bang.
(colloq.) The Big One.
(superl.) The Biggest One.
(accus.) You ruin *everything!*
(educ.) A Bunch of Children Left Behind.
(ant.) Gussying it all up.
(syn.) Dressing down, down to your bones.
(onomat.) *Pow! Crash! Pkwww!*
(naut.) Walk the plank.
(paleontol.) Caught between a rock and a hard place. Forever.
(agric.) Too many clear blue skies.
(K.J.V. Job 18:12) His strength shall be hungerbitten, and it shall be ready at his side.
(pseud.) Cap'n Catastrophe.
(euphem.) Pervasive lack of upkeep.
(interj.) Shitballs!
(bibl.) Horsemen come a-ridin'.
(univ.) This pomo moment has been shattered for you by Derrida.
(masc.) You wanna take this outside?
(fem.) Bitch bitch bitch.
(derog.) Unless you weren't really a fan of all that *order* to begin with.
(Confed.) You say *United*, we say, *Y'all's states.*
(meteorol.) We do this every day.
(mil.) We got you beat.
(fut.) Time to disarm, little big boys.
(dimin.) Bomblette.
(d.) Universe smooshed into a suitcase.

People Are Saying Things Again

people are saying things about
Canada & France & Argentina

maybe los desaparecidos = us
quizás, quizás, quizás. . . .

maybe the host grandma
calling me *pura americana*

maybe the Island School
maybe baby

it's time to zip up yr bags
& come home

to my folk song
where the nights are felted

with plenty of gutters
to do the catchwork

while I smash my cheek
hot to the window

to show the world
I care what's next

Notes & Acknowledgments

Poems Are the Only Real Bodies
Cover photo by Sean Patrick Cain.
Sections of this work appeared in *Poemeleon's* Epistolary Issue.

scenes from the lives of my parents
Cover illustration is public domain, from the *Voynich Manuscript*, a "scientific or magical text in an unidentified language, in cipher," carbon-dated to the 15th Century, with color botanical and astrological illustrations throughout. Held at the Beinecke Rare Book and Library Manuscript at Yale. For more information, see: <http://brbl-dl.library.yale.edu/vufind/Record/3519597>

Sources
Esterházy, Péter. *Celestial Harmonies.*
Singh, Simon. *The Code Book*.
Duffy, Eamon. *Marking the Hours: English People and Their Prayers.*
Parker-Pope, Tara. "The Science of a Happy Marriage." Well. *New York Times.*
   http://well.blogs.nytimes.com/2010/05/10/tracking-the-science-of-commitment/
Benson, Robert Louis. "Introduction."
   VENONA Historical Monograph #2: The 1942–43 New York–Moscow KGB Messages.
   http://www.theblackvault.com/documents/nsa/venona/monographs/monograph-2.html
Cassidy, Tina. *Birth: The Surprising History of How We are Born.*
D'Imperio, Mary E. *The Voynich Manuscript: An Elegant Enigma.*
   Available as a PDF from the NSA here:
   http://www.nsa.gov/about/cryptologic_heritage/center_crypt_history/publications/misc.shtml
Shakespeare, William. *Hamlet.*
Kenney, Padraic. *A Carnival of Revolution: Eastern Europe 1989.*
Kundera, Milan. *The Book of Laughter & Forgetting.*
Ould, Fielding. *A Treatise of Midwifery in Three Parts.*
Thomas, Pauline Weston. "Mourning Fashion / Fashion History."
   http://www.fashion-era.com/mourning_fashion.htm

Various. "Russian Spy Ring (2010)." Times Topics. *New York Times.*
http://topics.nytimes.com/top/reference/timestopics/subjects/r/russian_spy_ring_2010/index.html

Windowboxing: A Dance with Saints in Three Acts
Drawings by Koen Kaschock-Marenda.
Excerpts from this work appeared in *Antioch Review*, *BOMB Magazine*, *Chicago Review*, *Everyday Genius*, *Mad Hatters' Review*, *Many Mountains Moving*, and *Otoliths*.

Nonstop Pop
These poems were inspired by television, movies, music, pop culture, politics, shopping, the internet, America, and other poems. The italicized section of "On the Night Before TV Goes Digital" comes from a blog post on *Harriet* by Eileen Myles about Steve Carey. "Definition of Destruction" borrows the form of Matthea Harvey's "Definition of Weather." "More Lyrics for My Favorite Band": my favorite band is Destroyer. "Insurgent Country" was inspired by the film *Jesus Camp*. All the text from "Living the Secret" comes from the testimonial section of the same name on the website for the book *The Secret*, thesecret.tv. "Less Finesse, More Spank" is for Tasia Milton. The sentences from "The Superlatively Derogatory Colloquial Epithet, *Shammy*" come from *OED Online*'s sample sentences for a superlatively derogatory colloquial epithet. The text of "No Country for Young Ladies" and "I Was a Water Ballerina" was culled from the internet.

Excerpts first appeared in *Columbia Poetry Review*, *DIAGRAM*, *Eleven Eleven*, *Ghost Proposal*, *Finery*, *InDigest*, *JetFuel Review*, *Somnambulist Quarterly*, and *Super Arrow*.

About the Authors

Hailey Higdon is the author of the chapbooks *Packing* (Bloof Books, 2012), *How To Grow Almost Everything* (Agnes Fox, 2011) and the book-blog *The Palinode Project*. She runs What To Us (press). She is affiliated with many states and has many homes. She is a lifelong student of sound and language.

Kirsten Kaschock is the author of three books of poetry: *The Dottery* (Pitt), *Unfathoms* (Slope Editions) and *A Beautiful Name for a Girl* (Ahsahta Press). Her debut novel, *Sleight*, a work of speculative fiction, was published by Coffee House Press. She has earned a PhD in English from the University of Georgia and a PhD in dance from Temple University. Kirsten resides in Philadelphia with Dan Marenda and their three children. More at kaschock.wordpress.com.

Becca Klaver is the author of the poetry collection *LA Liminal* (Kore Press, 2010) and several chapbooks, including *Merrily, Merrily* (Lame House Press, 2013) and *Nonstop Pop* (Bloof Books, 2013). She holds a BA from the University of Southern California and an MFA from Columbia College Chicago and is completing her PhD in English at Rutgers University. She is a founding editor of Switchback Books, coeditor of *Electric Gurlesque*, and coeditor of the new feminist website WEIRD SISTER. With Lauren Besser, she co-hosts *The Real Housewives of Bohemia* podcast. Born and raised in Milwaukee, WI, she lives in Bed-Stuy.

Pattie McCarthy's most recent book is *Nulls*, published in 2014 by Horse Less Press. She is also the author of *Marybones, bk of (h)rs, Verso*, and *Table Alphabetical of Hard Words*, all from Apogee Press. Her chapbook *L&O* was published in 2011 by Little Red Leaves. A 2011 Pew Fellow in the Arts, she teaches literature and creative writing at Temple University.

Jennifer Tamayo is a writer and performer. She is the author of the hybrid collection of poems and art, *Red Missed Aches Read Missed Aches Red Mistakes Read Mistakes*, winner of the Gatewood Prize (Switchback, 2011) and *You Da One* (Coconut, 2014). JT serves as the Managing Editor at Futurepoem. She lives in Harlem.

Jared White's other chapbooks include *YELLOWCAKE*, published in the *Narwhal* anthology from Cannibal Books in 2009, and *MY FORMER POLITICS* from H_NGM_N in 2013. With Farrah Field, he is co-owner of a small press bookstore, Berl's Brooklyn Poetry Shop.

Index of Authors, Titles & First Lines

Individual pieces within this volume are listed alphabetically by title, or by first line if the piece does not bear a title. First lines or titles that appear more than once are followed by a second distinguishing line as a subentry: This is what it is like to be loved by me / again. *Titles are alphabetized by first word, excluding articles:* Stone That Produces Milk, The.

[ABANDANCE]   96

Amarinta,   38

Any Day Bill   109

Apple Bottoms Etc. When You Are Ready the Conversation Is Waiting   111

Araminta,   17

[ASKEDANCERED]   91

A the Beaut   156

Boho Wrapper   180

B®and Loyalty   165

[CELLARDANCE]   82

[CROWDEADANCE]   87

[DANCELLULAR]   73

[DANCESTRAL]   102

Dear Harriet,   20

Dear Harriet Tubman,
  How is it to be buried under the singular displeasure of the sentence?   16
  I want to use your body for my own pleasures.   18

Dear Moses,   25

Dear Mrs. Tubman,   37

Definition of Destruction   182

Direct Address   159

Everything Matters   120

Experience starts with the guh.   34

Foxy   166

Harriet,
    my clit perks and waves to the sun!   23
    Please excuse, I'm trying to arc at the moment   26
    This is a poem I did not write: 35
Harryette Mullen,   27
HIGDON, HAILEY   105–22
I know for certain   33
Image Union   167
Insurgent Country   171
It's Dark or Whatever You Call It   107
I Was a Water Ballerina   173
KASCHOCK, KIRSTEN   66–103
KLAVER, BECCA   151–83
Less Finesse, More Spank   175
Living the Secret   168
McCARTHY, PATTIE   41–63
Monday Pizza $9.99   162
More Lyrics for My Favorite Band   153
Moses,   29
New, Not Blue   158
No Country for Young Ladies   170
On the Night Before TV Goes Digital   154
Packed   110
Pavarotti Lip-Synched Last Performance   160
People Are Saying Things Again   183
Plot Point Two   172
P.S.   32
Red Arrow Down   178
[SAINTACTONE]   101
[SAINTHREE]   76
[SAINTWO]   93

*scenes from the lives of my parents
   & boy meets girl—he is a lifeguard—she is reading   55
   curtains swell from the windows & fill   60
   he was dressed like a smurf (it made the protest   61
   libel & the matter   56
   my father shaved his head in order to write   44
   my mother asked the midwife to place   50
   on your way to the mess hall a truck   45
   palimpsest   58
   secondly, that the body, taking in the shoulders, makes still   62
   Shakespeare makes the closet scene more dramatic by including the   54
   she said   46
   she said I love you   52
   she said nice hands   43
   she said to whom do you speak this?   53
   she was coming back from a break—two agents   49
   shibboleth   48
   they arrived on the SS Willehad in Fells Point, Baltimore on 4/11/07.   59
   they met in the first Voynich study group (1944–46) in which text was   51
   they were old school—messages   63
   when I was six I played by myself & drank   57
   when presented with the word puzzles   47
Schwarzeneggery   164
So Many Churches for Sale. Moving? Why Building?   114
Stone That Produces Milk, The   118
Superlatively Derogatory Colloquial Epithet, *Shammy*, The   176
TAMAYO, JENNIFER   13–38
That sentence can sustain all this   28
There's a terror that we will love   36
30 Years Happy Birthday Anyway   122

This is what it is like to be loved by me
   again.   143
   amoeba prokaryote goo in a stew of organic compounds.   140
   A poem of only observation and you observing   127
   as best as I can tell based on what it has been like to be   141
   as daily practice.   140
   asking a question that is supposed to be answered with   140
   as Rimbaud said—You's another.   133
   but I'm not me!   146
   by my beard hairs, which are longer than usual, growing   139
   carrying around a tiny container of nutella which I don't   132
   chaos and anarchy, freedom and bliss, two versions of the   146
   danger danger every itch feels reasonable.   144
   driving over the edge of the corniche and floating in the   137
   if my breath went down into my stomach and my food   128
   in a dark forest midway through my life.   134
   in another city where decisions turn into money and Peer   128
   in a pool on the seam where the shallow end meets the   130
   in the Odyssey when most of the time in the epic is   142
   in the periphery, everywhere your eye is, isn't.   135
   I say as the spotlight I shine in the mirror illuminates   142
   Judaism.   137
   once the light that cut through the fog has stopped cutting   130
   on the edge of the ocean or in the middle of the ocean,   136
   on the run.   138
   on the Trans-Siberian Railway, which takes six days to   143
   question mark   136
   summed up in a single word that is neither adjective nor   147
   thising and ising and whating and inging.   145
   total Romeo total Peer.   132

 translated from grammar into arithmetic and agriculture. 133
 under many ticking clocks, for there are many clocks if 138
 wait, wait, deletions. 131
 what it's like to be what it is like. 137
 writing a poem of not you. 129

What is happening here is a positioning: 15

When 115

WHITE, JARED 125–148

Why Not Minot 113

[WINDEED] 78

[WINDONEWITH] 94

[WINDON'T] 95

[WINDOORS] 75

[WINDORMANT] 77

[WINDOUBTFILLED] 85

[WINDOWAKING] 98

[WINDOWALK] 100

[WINDOWER] 69

[WINDOWNER] 72

[WINDOWNFALL] 89

[WINDOWØMEN] 71

[WINDOWRIGHT] 81

[WINDOWTREATMENT] 84

[WINNUENDO] 79

Windows are what make domesticity seem picturesque, in that windows make sculpture 70

Your art controls you by bringing up private 24

Your art controls you by putting you down all the 22

Your art controls your emotions by using body 31

Your art withholds information from you, and 19

Catalog & Chronology

Bloof Books (2007–2015)

A Gringo Like Me by Jennifer L. Knox
Drunk by Noon by Jennifer L. Knox
For Girls (& Others) by Shanna Compton
My Zorba by Danielle Pafunda
Warsaw Bikini by Sandra Simonds
Poetry! Poetry! Poetry! by Peter Davis
The Mystery of the Hidden Driveway by Jennifer L. Knox
Brink by Shanna Compton
TINA by Peter Davis
Natural History Rape Museum by Danielle Pafunda
Ultramegaprairieland by Elisabeth Workman
The Sonnets by Sandra Simonds
Days of Shame & Failure by Jennifer L. Knox
Greetings from My Girly Leisure Place by Sharon Mesmer
The Hazard Cycle by Shanna Compton

Chapbook Series

2013

Packing by Hailey Higdon
This Is What It Is Like to Be Loved by Me by Jared White
Nonstop Pop by Becca Klaver
Poems Are the Only Real Bodies by Jennifer Tamayo
Windowboxing by Kirsten Kaschock
scenes from the lives of my parents by Pattie McCarthy

2014

Odalisque by Ben Fama
The Failure Age by Amanda Montei
Conversation with the Stone Wife by Natalie Eilbert
Little Uglies by Dawn Sueoka
Bedtime Stories for the End of the World! by Daniel Borzutzky
Sympathethic Nervous System by Jackie Clark

2015

The Woman, the Mirror, the Eye by Maureen Thorson
Hymn: An Ovulation by Jenn Marie Nunes & Mel Coyle
Knotted by Alyssa Lynee
Exercises in Painting by Khadijah Queen
First the Burning & Then the Witches by Catie Rosemurgy
Inherit by Ginger Ko
I Hate Telling You How I Really Feel by Nikki Wallschlaeger

Anthologies

Bound: Volume One
Bound: Volume Two

www.ingramcontent.com/pod-product-compliance
Lightning Source LLC
Chambersburg PA
CBHW080412170426
43194CB00015B/2791